Ordinary Grace

Ordinary Grace

An Examination of the Roots of
Compassion, Altruism, and
Empathy, and the Ordinary
Individuals Who Help Others in
Extraordinary Ways

KATHLEEN A. BREHONY

Riverhead Books

a member of

Penguin Putnam Inc.

New York

1999

Riverhead Books
a member of
Penguin Putnam Inc.
375 Hudson Street
New York, NY 10014

A list of permissions can be found on page 241.

Library of Congress Cataloging-in-Publication Data

Brehony, Kathleen A.
Ordinary grace: an examination of the roots of compassion,
altruism, and empathy, and the ordinary individuals who help
others in extraordinary ways / Kathleen A. Brehony.
p. cm.
Includes bibliographical references.
ISBN 1-57322-108-2 (alk. paper)
1. Helping behavior. 2. Helping behavior—Case studies. 3. Caring.
4. Altruism. 5. Empathy. I. Title.
BF637.H4B74   1999   98-31876 CIP
177'.7—dc21

Printed in the United States of America

1   3   5   7   9   10   8   6   4   2

This book is printed on acid-free paper. ♾

BOOK DESIGN BY CHRIS WELCH

This book is dedicated to the memory of Steve Ross,
a man of true grace, whom I never knew—
except through my heart.

Unformed people delight in the gaudy and in novelty.
Cooked people delight in the ordinary.
—Zen saying

Contents

Ordinary Grace

Introduction

The Perception of Good and Evil—whatever choice we
may make—is the first requisite of spiritual life.

—T. S. Eliot, *After Strange Gods*

Sixty-nine-year-old Thomas Cannon lives in a poor, run-down neighborhood in Richmond, Virginia. Retired from the Postal Service and living on only $12,000 a year from Social Security and a meager pension, he takes care of his wife, Princetta, who is bedridden following the devastating effects of a stroke. On the surface, Thomas Cannon's life seems ordinary. But since 1972, he has given away a total of $81,000 to eighty-one strangers, each of whom he considered deserving of a thousand-dollar gift.

The first check was donated to a women's club that provided help and support to young children at an underfunded elementary school. Other donations over the years have gone to a paralyzed man, a Vietnamese boy who struggled to support his impoverished parents, a twelve-year-old girl who works with the homeless, and the widow of a police officer who died in the line of duty. He once sent a check to a millionaire philanthropist who had acted heroically. Each check is sent with a note describing why the gift is being sent and thanking the recipient for his or her contribution to a better world. "Each check," he says, "is merely a symbol of my love and caring for that individual. There are some very deserving people in this world and my gifts are my way of recognizing what they do."[1]

Eunice Lewis works as a certified nursing assistant for handicapped and elderly people who require help with their daily needs. She cooks and cleans for them, she helps them get dressed, buttoning buttons and smoothing out wrinkles when weakened fingers can no longer manage. Eunice lives an ordinary life and has an ordinary job, but she brings extraordinary grace to her work when she sings. Her voice is reminiscent of Anita Baker's, and her faith in the power of music is deep. "I noticed that when I sang to my people, they seemed to feel much better—happier, comforted," she says. "So I sing to them every day."[2]

Sharon Trenkle and Patricia Ann Sill are unlikely best friends. These women's lives changed forever when, on a cold evening just a few weeks before Christmas of 1992, Sharon's son Jamie walked into the house of his former girlfriend, Patricia Ann's daughter Amy. He sprayed the house with bullets, killing Amy and wounding her mother. With tears streaming down his face he said, "I'm sorry," and then killed himself with a bullet to his head. Given the magnitude of these two mothers' losses, common sense tells us that they should be bitter enemies. But there is no rancor between them. Rising above the pain of their tragedy, they have learned to heal their grief by leaning on each other and trusting in their bond of compassion and friendship. Together they lobby the state and federal legislatures for gun control. Together they visit their children's graves at Rosewood Memorial Park Cemetery. "God has a reason for everything," says Patricia Ann, one hand grasping the locket around her neck that contains a baby picture of her daughter, and the other squeezing Sharon's hand. "I couldn't ask for a better friend," Sharon says. "She's always been there."[3]

What is this grace that allows acts of seemingly impossible generosity from a poor man or kindness beyond the call of duty from a woman in an underpaid, undervalued job? From what miraculous well of the human spirit does pure forgiveness flow, after great tragedy? And what can the lives and beliefs of these people teach us about our own capacity to enact sacredness in our everyday lives?

Richard Hassell travels the streets of Tidewater, Virginia, in an old beat-up car, searching for the homeless, the downtrodden, the needy. He gives them hot meals, puts them in motels for the night, often at his own expense, and then picks them up the next morning and takes them to a nearby Social Services office to help them find permanent shelter and financial aid. He's been doing this, day and night, since the 1940s. What brings Richard Hassell out day after day?

Are these people's acts the result of extraordinary circumstances, or of the influence of special teachers? Do all such people act merely out of the conviction that their deeds will be rewarded in an afterlife?

We seldom hear through the media about good works like these. Instead, the news that floods our television screens and daily papers is filled with horrific, inhuman, and evil doings; yet another murder, robbery, rape, or immoral abuse of power. The media seem to focus on the dark side of human nature and to follow the axioms "If it bleeds, it leads," and "Good news is no news."

Made aware of so much evil, we have become numbed by it. Many of us are no longer outraged or even surprised by heinous acts. Every day the media feed us information that confirms our collective belief that our culture is a dangerous one. Acts of random violence, lack of trust, and the feeling that people are exclusively in pursuit of their own self-interests surround us daily. And for the most part, the people who behave in immoral and violent ways are just as ordinary as those who act out of generosity or kindness. Apart from the depraved act that has plucked them from their daily lives and put them onto the front page, they are not extraordinary people. Just like Thomas Cannon, Eunice Lewis, and Richard Hassell, they live in houses that we pass as we drive through our cities. They work at stores in which we shop. They fix our cars, install new storm windows in our attic dormers, or sell us life insurance. They are ordinary people, and many of them are more like us than we care to believe.

A few years ago, I was surfing through the television channels when I came upon a documentary about Adolf Hitler. The image on the screen was not Hitler as I had seen him in other film clips: forcefully orating in front of a microphone or giving the Nazi salute from an elaborate reviewing stand. Instead, this was Hitler in a field with two dogs. He threw a stick for one, and when the dog returned it Hitler knelt down and patted his head. There was no sound, but it was clear that he was smiling and talking to the dog. I was struck by the thought that the most horrific depravity resided in a human being who could attend to his dogs with what appeared to be love.

Hannah Arendt, who was the first to arrive at the theory of the banality of evil, described in great detail the ways in which evil can exist in the hearts of average people as she followed Nazi leader Adolf Eichmann's trial in Nuremberg in 1961. Prosecutors in Jerusalem used all their resources to attempt to expose Eichmann's extraordinary evil, to reveal him as a monster, as they questioned him about his role in the Holocaust. Arendt wrote, "The trouble with Eichmann was precisely that so many were like him, and that the many were neither perverted, nor sadistic, that they were, and still are, terribly and terrifyingly normal."[4]

We are surrounded by evil every day, and like amateur sociologists we can plot the trajectories leading to almost any unspeakable act: histories of poverty, drug abuse, broken homes, eroded values, alienation, and insecurity. We can explain evil on many levels: genetics, biological determinants, internal psychological factors, and external sociological, economic, and cultural pressures. Most of us think we understand how all of these factors, both nature and nurture, can converge and contribute to the high levels of violence, dishonesty, and callousness that so often seem to characterize our society. While we may debate the relative importance of all these factors, one thing we do understand is that ordinary people can do unspeakable things.

But why do people do good deeds?

Is it more reasonable to accept that evil is ordinary but goodness is not? Because we are not accustomed to seeing goodness— kindness, compassion, generosity—portrayed on television and written about in newspapers, we can come to believe that it is a rare commodity. But for every instance of violence or greed there are thousands of acts of benevolence and tolerance. And many of the people who perform them have experienced some of the same debilitating effects of poverty, violence, and lack of healthy moral values as those who commit evil acts. Yet unlike those who succumb to those pressures, somehow they have forged grace from this refiner's fire. The truth is, we understand (or think we understand) far more about why people live lives filled with hatred than we do about why others bring forth the energies of love and compassion into our world. One reason for this disparity is that goodness often reveals itself quietly.

During the course of conducting interviews for this book, I attended a dinner in Norfolk, Virginia, to celebrate the contributions of volunteers. These people were from all walks of life, ages, and racial groups. I was particularly impressed by a sixteen-year-old boy, a tough-looking African-American kid who wore his hair in dreadlocks. Most of the people in the room would have been frightened if they'd met him in a bad part of town, given what our society has come to believe about young black men and their propensity for violence and crime. But here was a teenager who had devoted more than fifteen hundred hours in the past year to working with the elderly in our area. He delivered hot meals, ran errands for the housebound, and sat and talked with them when no one else would. Though it was neither the time nor the place, I wanted to ask him a great many questions. What drove him to help old people instead of pursuing what most people consider the inalienable rights of youth: sex, fun, and slacking off with friends? What were his experiences while growing up? Was he reared in a loving, nurturing environment? Had he had any special mentors or transforming experiences that caused him to act compassionately? Had his need to help others come to him in a sudden spiritual awakening, or had he always felt that way? Was he even conscious of the reasons behind his actions? From the information in the evening's program, I knew that he was from the same housing project as a group of teenage boys who had recently killed a man as he walked home from a baseball game. I speculated that by growing up where he did he must have experienced at least some of the same kinds of despair, violence, and temptations as the other boys had. Why is it that two people can have many of the same experiences and yet respond to life's challenges and opportunities in such different ways? As I thought about these questions, I looked around the room and was struck both by the sense of grace and love that surrounded me there and by the ordinariness of the people who had quietly brought this consciousness into our community.

There is a large and growing literature on the nature of values and virtue. But even a familiarity with the work of Lawrence Kohlberg, Carol Gilligan, and the countless others who have addressed the issues of moral development cannot answer all the questions. Are there everyday beliefs or experiences that give rise to compassion and generosity? What is the process of coming to grace? Does it emerge in some slow way, a simple devotion that at first appears arbitrary and insufficient, but which has a cumulative power for both the recipient and the giver of grace? Or is some transformative experience—an epiphany—required to begin the process? What is the larger spiritual context in which grace thrives? Why does a Lakota shaman feel the same desire to feed the homeless as does an evangelical Christian woman who speaks in tongues at the Rock Church?

I have always been fascinated by the concepts of good and evil; like many people, I had come to think of them as opposites: Some people are good, others are evil. But the truth is much murkier. As human beings we possess both light and shadow; we are capable of both good and evil. It is as Emerson wrote: "There is a capacity of virtue in us, and there is a capacity of vice to make your blood creep."[5]

If the potential for both goodness and evil resides in all

human beings, then surely it is at least as important to understand what leads us to goodness as it is to perceive the path to violence or evil. Whether banal or extraordinary, goodness surrounds us and we don't understand it. What is it that causes people to look beyond their bills and appointment books and make sacrifices; to act from a desire—even a need—to help others?

It may be that our philosophical, psychological, and spiritual literature can point in a general direction and help articulate the questions. But this book goes to the source. In it, I set out to know why people like those I have interviewed spend enormous time and energy in helping others, while so many other people, often with good intentions, are overwhelmed by the demands of everyday life. What allows the first group to live above and beyond the quotidian, and sustain their internal beliefs with compassionate and loving *action* in the world? What causes some people to transcend their everyday lives and (in some cases) their destructive backgrounds in their desire to bring kindness to the lives of others? By talking with and studying people who demonstrate ordinary grace in their lives, I discovered that goodness expresses itself in endless ways.

The stories that inform this book come from the lives of men and women of all races, ages, creeds, and lifestyles. They are rich and poor, able-bodied and disabled. They live in large cities and small towns. They are not perfect human beings, nor are they saints on earth. They are simply people who have found a deep generosity within themselves, and the courage and energy to put it to good use. Perhaps by understanding what makes people draw on the good in themselves, by taking these stories into our hearts, we can look into our own lives more deeply and feel inspired to take action. Imagine how the world would be different if we all embodied Margaret Mead's most compelling admonition: "Don't believe that even a small group of committed people cannot change the world. It's the only thing that ever has."

1.

Awakening to Ordinary Grace

To know the good is to do the good.

—Plato

M y interest in studying what makes people express goodness goes back a long way. As a graduate student in psychology in 1978, I worked with Professor Scott Geller at Virginia Tech. I couldn't have asked for a better dissertation chairman: Scott is an extremely bright, creative, conscientious man whose regard for his students as younger colleagues gave us the confidence to explore our own questions. In addition to his considerable academic skills and prolific publication in scientific journals, he also has musical talent—as a drummer. With two other graduate students, we started a rock-and-roll band.

Scott is a first-rate musician—he once sat in with the Kingsmen (remember "Louie, Louie"?) on a summer tour when their regular drummer was unavailable. Jeff Aston, our lead guitarist, and Mark Albert, the bass player, were also excellent musicians. I'm more of a three-chords-and-go rhythm guitar player, but because we concentrated our repertoire on songs from the fifties and sixties, my lack of musical accomplishment went largely unnoticed. Anyone who has played the music of that era knows that with a little stage presence, you can easily get away with playing the same three chords indefinitely.

We had an intermittent schedule of gigs—mostly graduate student parties—but one summer we were asked to perform at Camp Easter Seals, a program that was part of a research project Scott and some of his students were undertaking. The camp was for children with special challenges; most of them had severe mental or physical disabilities. The camp counselors were students from Virginia Tech earning degrees in psychology or education, and their summer at the camp gave them real-life experience in working with special children.

It was during that summer at Camp Easter Seals that I began to notice goodness in new ways. I had always been aware of acts of kindness or generosity, but something that summer caused a profound change in my perception of them, a paradigm shift. Marcel Proust observed that "the real voyage of discovery consists not in seeking new landscapes, but in having new eyes." I was beginning to learn how different the world looks with even a subtle shift in perception.

A dance was scheduled for Friday night at the camp, and our

band was invited to play. To these children, we were the real thing—we all wore sunglasses and dressed like rock stars. The student counselors had decorated the dining hall with balloons and crêpe paper. Refreshments were served—punch and cake—and it was a genuine dance party. In their innocence and their excitement about having live music, these kids couldn't have cared less that our microphones were attached to their stands with duct tape or that our sound equipment was a hodge-podge of amplifiers and speakers taken from our home stereos and whatever we could beg from the audio-visual department at Virginia Tech. They didn't even notice that almost every song sounded a lot like the one before it. They were thrilled by the loud music and the opportunity to dance. They cheered and screamed after all of the songs and often throughout them. One little girl asked for my autograph and told me that, except for Linda Ronstadt, I was her favorite singer in the world.

As we opened our second set, I watched as a twelve-year-old boy with Down's syndrome walked toward a younger boy in a wheelchair. I knew that the little guy, Danny, was severely retarded, blind, and totally deaf. He had been sitting quietly on the edge of the dancing crowd. The twelve-year-old went behind him and wheeled his chair directly in front of Scott's drums, and as soon as he did this, Danny's expression changed: he began to smile. He reached out his hand and pressed it against the vibrating bass drum. Then he laughed out loud—what he could not hear, he could *feel.* Soon every child in the room was standing close to Danny, dancing, laughing, and touching him on the head and shoulders. They never left his side for the rest of the night.

I have no idea how a young boy with Down's syndrome realized that Danny's deafness kept him separated from the rest of the group. I don't understand how he figured out that the beating drum could be a doorway through which that little boy could enter the party. Somehow, intuitively, he knew things that even the well-meaning camp counselors didn't. The party became a magical expression of the deep connections that can be felt when we open our hearts. Our band never sounded better than it did that night.

The next morning, I watched the interaction between "Big" David, a Virginia Tech sophomore and "Little" David, a ten-year-old boy who was born without arms or legs. Little David's father was a military officer; he and David's mother had lived in Germany during the first trimester of their son's development. David's mother had taken the sedative Thalidomide during her pregnancy before it was known that this drug causes severe problems for a developing fetus. David was one of only a few American babies born with birth defects caused by the drug, since it was never distributed in the United States. In Europe, where the drug was legal, approved, and widely used, thousands of children were born with these same deformities.

In place of arms and legs, Little David had small "flippers," which allowed him to grasp objects but kept him in a wheelchair. Despite his enormous physical challenges, he had no problems with his intellectual abilities. He was very bright and naturally curious. In spite of the great differences in their physical abilities, Big David and Little David had the same sense of humor and became good friends. They shared a strong interest in the natural world, and Big David, who was earning a minor in biology, answered hundreds of questions from Little David about the trees and flowers at the camp. The two of them talked for hours about how the Blue Ridge Mountains were formed, and whether bears are completely asleep when they hibernate.

Later that morning, Big David asked to talk to me. "I want to take Little David on a hike so he can see the camp from the top of that ridge over there," he said, pointing halfway up the mountain. I wasn't sure how that would be possible. Little David couldn't walk, and even though he was a small child he would be too heavy to be carried all that way.

"He really wants to do it and I've figured out a way," Big David told me.

"Are you certain that he'll be safe?" I asked him.

"Absolutely." Big David was a hiker and rock climber in excellent physical condition, and he knew the trails that led to the ridge. Even at eighteen, he had a level of maturity and judgment that led me to trust him.

A few minutes later I saw them at the edge of the camp, starting up the trail to the ridge. Little David was riding in a backpack, the kind with an aluminum frame that allows hikers to distribute weight and carry heavy loads for long distances. He was strapped on Big David's back, his flippers holding an Audubon book that identified plants and flowers. He was smiling and excited, just like any boy about to embark on the adventure of exploring mountain trails with his good friend.

It was the ease of this moment that seemed to me so filled with grace. As I watched the two Davids disappear into the woods, I was aware of how ordinary their adventure was. Natural compassion had shown itself simply: just two young guys solving the problem of getting one of them to the top of a hill. They were both happy and excited to have figured it out, and once they'd done so, they simply proceeded with their day. And yet it is precisely because grace occurs in such ordinary settings and in such ordinary people that it is so easily overlooked.

We all make decisions about what we will emphasize as we live our lives. Whether we "tune in" and open our hearts to ordinary grace or not is a personal choice. And we make these decisions on matters both profound and mundane. On the highway, do we focus on the driver who cuts us off with a rude gesture, or do we notice, instead, the trucker who slows down a little to let us onto the expressway? Do we hold the door open for the person behind us coming into a store, or do we just keep going?

In 1986, I experienced a collective sense of grace when I was producing a video program for the Special Olympics. These athletic games are for people with physical and mental disabilities, and emphasize doing one's best and having fun rather than competition. During a half-mile race, one young girl lagged far behind the others. As the rest of the athletes were about to cross the finish line, the teenage girl who was in the lead looked back and saw how far behind the little girl was. She immediately turned around and ran toward her, as did all the other runners. These young athletes, of many races and ages, gathered on the track and kept pace with the little girl, all the while telling her she could make it. They crossed the finish line in a pack. In the several minutes it took to complete the race, all the spectators rose to their feet, clapping and cheering. The young runners had taught us a magnificent lesson about compassion, and an indescribable feeling surged through the crowd like an electric current.

I experienced the power of grace, friendship, and love again when I attended a collective eightieth-birthday party, sponsored by United Way of the Virginia Peninsula, for the volunteers of RSVP, the Retired and Senior Volunteer Program.[1] This program offers volunteering opportunities to people fifty-five and older throughout the United States, many of whom work with Meals on Wheels, with programs to feed the hungry, and with literacy and mentoring services for young people. Others visit nursing homes and care for other elderly people. Some of the women are "baby rockers," who volunteer at hospitals to sit and rock ill or irritable infants through the night. Last year, people associated with RSVP donated more than eighty million hours of help to communities across the nation—a service that has been estimated to be worth more than a billion dollars.

The birthday luncheon was a gala affair. A disc jockey played country music and a square-dance club entertained us—the theme was a country hoe-down and everyone wore a colorful bandanna. Meat loaf, mashed potatoes, corn muffins, and desserts were served by businessmen and by women from a local Rotary Club. "I always love to see those guys here in their beautiful three-piece suits," said Paula Ogiba, the volunteer coordinator for RSVP. "I always say, 'Take off those jackets, boys, 'cause you're gonna sweat!'"

I watched as these elderly people, both black and white, some moving spryly, others using walkers and canes, helped one another across thresholds and sat with their arms around one another. Every one of them had lived through more than eighty years of American history, and many had witnessed firsthand the extraordinary upheaval of the twentieth century. They all told me essentially the same things about why they spend time volunteering: "It's an honor to help other people because we're all really the same," "Everyone should help out in their community—how else will things get done?" and "I just love people." They spoke about the gifts and benefits they received rather than what they were giving. Many had come from desperately poor families themselves, and spoke about how they never wanted to see someone else go hungry or without shelter. A few spoke of their religious beliefs as the foundation of their compassion.

I talked with eighty-two-year-old Dorothy Feeback and her one-hundred-year-old mother, Avenel Salyer. Avenel was born in Ohio and raised in the coal fields of Kentucky, in a family that she says was rich in love but not in much else. She took my hand and told me that she thought it was a fine idea to try to understand why people do good things because in her century of living she'd seen the benefits of helping others. "I can't hardly hear you, honey," she said over the loud music. "But I can tell you that you can't live very well all on your own. You have to know how to live with other people and the more we help each other the better off everyone is. I'm going to keep on doing that until I'm no longer able."

Avenel Salyer's sense of connection to others and her wisdom about people helping each other out is a philosophy that resonates with forty-two-year-old Wayne Kelly. In 1991, the National Marrow Donor Program Registry, with more than two and a half million names, identified him as a potential match for twenty-two-year-old Don Creighton, who was dying of acute leukemia. Later tests confirmed that Wayne was a "perfect" six-antigen marrow match, extremely rare among nonrelatives. Bone marrow is the only donated organ that must correspond at the level of DNA in order to be transplanted, and the increasing incidence of diseases like leukemia, aplastic anemia, and lymphomas means that more and more bone marrow donors will be needed in the future. At any given moment, there are more than two thousand active searches of the NMDP Registry—and two thousand people whose lives hang in the balance. Thirty to forty people die every day because no match has been found. These patients often have a greater chance of winning a national lottery than of finding an able donor in time.[2]

Wayne Kelly never thought twice about going through with the procedure. A former firefighter who was critically injured when a two-story brick wall fell on his back, he was told he would never walk again. After several years of physical therapy and many prayers, he did. He understands something important about the human spirit and the will to live and to thrive. "I can't imagine the anchor that it would place on my heart to know that I could help someone fighting for his life and not do everything that I could," he told me. "It would be just like driving past an accident and not stopping. We're here to help each other, aren't we?"

Over the past seven years, Wayne Kelly and Don Creighton have become great friends. Even after their first telephone conversation, they felt as if they had known each other all their lives, and since then, they have discovered many shared interests. Wayne says that Don always asks what he can do to repay the gift he was given by a stranger. Wayne tells him that it is he who has been blessed by the opportunity to help someone else. "There is only one way to go forward from here," Wayne told him. "That is to live."

Against all the odds, Wayne was called upon again to donate bone marrow, but said he had a "bad feeling" because the recipient was so sick that they rescheduled the procedure four times. This patient was not as lucky as Don Creighton and died two months after receiving Wayne's marrow. Although he had never met this man, and in fact only knew his first name, Wayne did not feel like a stranger, and was devastated when he was told the news. In spite of this heartache, Wayne continues to keep himself on the donor list. "It's a blessing to be able to help someone in this way. Don is a parole officer and helps a lot of young people. There is a ripple effect in helping another," he says.

What we believe about the world shapes what we see. Because negativity and evil are present in the world, our worst fears and expectations are often easily confirmed. Our experiences reinforce our beliefs, and thus we cling even tighter to those beliefs. The same holds true for ordinary grace. We will see what we expect to see. As William Blake so eloquently wrote, "If the doors of perception were cleansed everything would appear to man as it is, infinite."[3] Once you understand that this grace is ever-present, you know that the experience of it is only a breath away.

The people with whom I talked and traveled, and who told me their stories, represent the full spectrum of human beings. They range in age from very young children to a one-hundred-year-old woman who continues to volunteer for community service. They are rich, poor, and in between, and represent a diversity of races, ethnic groups, sexual orientations, and lifestyles. Some follow paths based on strong religious beliefs, others describe themselves as "spiritual but not religious," and quite a few declare that they are not at all religious or spiritual-minded. These people come from major cities, small towns, and rural areas all over the country. I could have found enough ordinary grace in any one village to write a hundred books.

The stories confirm the abundant presence of grace in the world, but most important, they serve as examples of how we can choose to live. Psychologists refer to "modeling"—doing what we see others doing—as one of the major ways in which people learn. Buddhism speaks of the importance of "companioned example" and "Right Association" as preliminary steps on the "Eightfold Path" to enlightenment. It is said that when taming and training a wild elephant, the best way to start is by yoking it to one already tamed.[4] As you read the stories that follow, you may begin to realize that these people are no different from you. Knowing about them can awaken our own generous instincts for goodness, and impart the wisdom that we have the power to make the world a better place. As I write these stories and think about the people I've seen—Big David, Wayne Kelly, and Avenel Salyer, and others like them—I am deeply moved. I believe that the feelings their actions stirred in me can be experienced by anyone. Mythologist Harold Goddard rightly observed that "the destiny of the world is determined less by the battles that are lost and won than by the stories it loves and believes in."[5]

2.

The Nature
of Goodness

Grace is nothing else but a certain beginning of glory in us.

—Thomas Aquinas, *Summa Theologica*

While taking an early morning walk one Sunday, I passed a small wooden church near Blacksburg, Virginia, and heard a man's voice booming from inside. As I slowed to listen, I could hear the preacher telling his congregation how difficult it would be for any of them ever to reach the gates of Heaven, since they were all so very evil. I wondered how the rest of the day would go for people who had started the morning with such a blasting. Those people are not alone; the idea that we are born without innate goodness has been the stuff of millions of sermons emphasizing the need for salvation and repentance, not only for our volitional acts but also for our very natures. It is a theme heard around the world.

From this perspective, moral development is not a matter of improving upon our basic goodness through *acts* of kindness or generosity, but is instead a movement away from our base natures and, in fact, from nature itself. The Christian ritual of baptism is meant to remove original sin just after birth and give Christians a fresh start to live a moral life, one that will lead to eternal salvation.[1] If we yearn for the gift of goodness, we are advised to move away from instinct, sensuality, and earthly pleasures.

The idea that human beings are innately brutish and sinful appears early in Western thought, and can be found in the Judeo-Christian creation story. In Genesis, man is a fallen creature and thus human nature is not to be trusted. Because Adam and Eve ate the forbidden fruit from the tree of knowledge, disobeying God's command, the rest of us must attempt to find salvation in the aftermath of this sin. The seriousness of Adam's expulsion from the Garden of Eden is reflected in Psalms 51:5: "Indeed, I was born guilty, a sinner when my mother conceived me." In the New Testament, St. Paul states: "Man is essentially broken," and "Sin dwells within me." St. Augustine labeled man's and woman's initial fall from grace "original sin," thus canonizing the idea that human beings are born sinful. Augustine argued that neither morality nor sexual desire was "natural" to man; rather, they had been instilled in humans by God as chastisement for Adam's and Eve's sin. Sexual desire and the facts of procreation were for Augustine proof of, and punishment for, this universal original sin which stains every human being born into the world.

This belief was strongly embraced during the Middle Ages,

during which Christian theologians elaborated on St. Augustine's thinking. *Confession of Faith,* a book written in 1560 for the Presbyterian Church of Scotland, states flatly, "By which transgression, commonly called Original Sin, was the image of God utterly defiled in man; and he and his posterity of nature become enemies to God, slaves to Satan, and servants to sin."[2]

Although other questionable dogmas arose during the Middle Ages, the idea of man's inherent evil never disappeared. Western philosophers of the Realist persuasion, such as Thomas Hobbes in the sixteenth century, emphasized the notion that humans are low creatures and that goodness can be imposed only by strict social laws. These beliefs resonated particularly well in American society, which was heavily influenced by Puritanical interpretations of Christian theology and by the rational arguments of the Realist school. Although there are many Judeo-Christian interpretations of the story of creation, the idea that human nature is basically corrupt permeates Western philosophy to this day. Elaine Pagels, a writer and professor of religion at Princeton University, describes the importance of Augustine's views to the early Christian Church in the establishment of its authority: "Augustine's theory of original sin not only proved politically expedient, since it persuaded many of his contemporaries that human beings universally need external government—which meant, in their case, both a Christian state and an imperially supported church—but also offered an analysis of human nature that became, for better and worse, the heritage of all subsequent generations of western Christians and the major influence on their psychological and political thinking."[3] Sigmund Freud, in many ways the father of modern psychology, wrote extensively on the baseness of human nature, especially in children. For him, civilization was merely a means of putting limitations on the immoderate, aggressive, selfish aims of human nature.[4]

The basic assumption that human beings are born without virtue continues to exert enormous influence over our present-day beliefs. William Bennett, an advocate for traditional/conservative values and the author of the recent, popular tome, *The Book of Virtues,* makes this point very clearly. He writes: "The vast majority of Americans share a respect for certain fundamental traits of character: honesty, compassion, courage, and perseverance. These are virtues. But because children are not born with this knowledge, they need to learn what these virtues are."[5]

The point Bennett makes is that we have to *develop* a sense of goodness in order to live with grace, virtue, and, perhaps, God's love. No one would disagree with the idea that human behavior is ultimately a function of both nature *and* nurture, and that teaching and modeling moral values is essential for the fullest expression of human goodness. Nor would it be possible to neglect the observation that one of the functions of culture is to regulate human behavior through the creation and teaching of laws and values. Nevertheless, the assumption that human beings are born without virtue colors everything we believe about ourselves and others. Most important, it sets in motion a system of convictions that creates distrust and disrespect.

However, even though I too am aware of this influential understanding of human behavior, I can't help but think of certain moments in my life that suggest another way of looking at our basic natures.

As I was negotiating a narrow street while driving to work one day, I watched a mother putting her infant into a car seat. She had both the front and back doors of the car open, and as I slowed down to pass, I could see between the two open doors a little girl, maybe five or six years old, standing on the curb and holding her three-year-old younger brother in a tight bear hug. She kissed him on the top of his head, and I heard her say, "I've got you. Stay by me." It was a beautiful image of sibling love to start my day—a simple moment of ordinary grace.

This scene reminded me of my relationship with my own younger brother, Jimmy, and of one particular day when I was seven and he was five. My father had returned from a business trip to Cleveland and had brought us gifts, as he always did when his work took him out of town. He opened his suitcase and pulled out two coin banks made of plaster of Paris and covered with something resembling fur. Mine was a woeful-looking, dark-brown basset hound. Jimmy's was a red monkey with a bee on its nose and its eyes crossed, as if it were looking at the insect. They were wonderful presents and we loved them at first sight. Jimmy was so excited that he ran up the steps to show his gift to our dog. "Careful," my mother said. "That bank will break if you drop it."

The warning was prophetic, and within seconds he dropped

his bank. It rolled down the steps with a great clunking sound and cracked into hundreds of tiny pieces. He sat on the steps, head in hands, unable to cry out loud, being a boy in the 1950s and also having been amply warned. I saw his big blue eyes fill with tears. I sat next to him, kissed his cheek, and without even thinking, gave my dog bank to him. It was more important to me that he not feel so sad than to have a new bank myself. I remember the *feeling* very clearly: it hurt my heart to see him cry; his tears made me feel like crying too.

If one stops to consider what motivates such apparently simple acts of kindness between children, one might be surprised to encounter a number of questions that have been debated by philosophers, psychologists, religious scholars, and scientists for centuries. For example, is the fact that I gave my bank to my brother evidence that I was acting out of a kind and benevolent nature, one that I was born with, or does it merely suggest that my parents had succeeded in driving out the selfish impulses from my soul? The way that we answer this question has everything to do with how we understand ordinary grace.

There are many thinkers, both ancient and modern, who do not believe that humans are fundamentally flawed and basically evil. Plato taught that a person is the measure of all things and is born neither good nor bad, but rather is open to both possibilities, which can be imparted by experience and training. Heraclitus was similarly inclined, and suggested that human nature is capable of both good and evil and that these potentialities were like "two notes in a harmony."

Some philosophers and theologians have gone further with the belief that human beings are not born merely with equal capacities for good and evil but are, in fact, born innocent and good—a tangible representation of the love and creative spirit of God. There is no concept of "original sin" in Jewish tradition, for example, even though the Jewish people were exposed to the creation story of Genesis a thousand years before Christians were. In this view, the notion of evil as basic to human beings distorts the fact that all beings are *blessed*, having been created by a loving God, and that therefore our natural proclivity should be to love and care for one another. The idea that the nature of human beings is divine and that we are born with dignity and the full measure of God's love can be found in both the Old and New Testaments. In the Book of Psalms, an ancient Hebrew psalmist asks God about how God thinks of man, saying, "Thou hast made him a little lower than the angels, and hast crowned him with glory and honor." Although this view has been stated in many ways by philosophers, Eastern religious thinkers, and the oral traditions of many indigenous cultures, I particularly like the way it was illuminated by the twelfth-century Christian mystic Hildegard of Bingen: "Every creature," she elegantly wrote, "is a glimmering, glistening mirror of Divinity."[6]

On August 16, 1996, a three-year-old boy climbed over a stone-and-bamboo barrier at the Brookfield Zoo, in Brookfield, Illinois, and fell more than eighteen feet to the concrete floor of the Tropic World primate exhibit. As he lay there unconscious, he was approached by an eight-year-old female western lowland gorilla named Binti-Jua (Swahili for "daughter of sunshine"), who had her own baby, Koola, at her breast. Binti immediately picked the boy up, cradled him, and began to rock him. She kept the other animals away by making growling noises, and shielded the boy with her body. As she carried him across the compound, she stood up to a very aggressive, larger gorilla, and then gently set the boy down at the zookeepers' door, where she was accustomed to seeing human attendants. "You could tell, you could just feel she was going to help the boy," said Eric Allison, a tourist who was visiting the zoo. Within a few moments, the boy was retrieved by zoo personnel and off-duty paramedics and rushed to the hospital in critical condition. He made a quick recovery, and was discharged several days later with a broken hand, some minor cuts and bruises, and no memory of his ordeal.

Bob Allison, Eric's father, took pictures with his camera throughout the rescue of the boy. He described Binti's behavior as she approached the toddler: "She lifted his arm as if looking for signs of life. She did that twice. It seemed like she was asking, 'Are you OK?' Then she lifted the boy and put him to her chest, just exactly the way she was holding her own baby." Bob Allison's amazing photographs capturing Binti's compassion were published in several national magazines and have been seen throughout the world.

In the analyses that followed the worldwide reporting of this story, many noted that Binti is not exactly a *wild* lowland gorilla. She was raised in a zoo, after all, and had been taken away from her own mother as an infant and cared for by zoo personnel. "Would Binti have acted any differently if she had been handling, say, a sack of flour?" a researcher asked in the *San Francisco Examiner.* Bob Allison agrees that it is impossible to know exactly what was going on in her mind. Still, he is convinced that her intentions were compassionate. He often looks at his photographs in search of clues: "I keep studying them, studying her face and her posture. I can't help but think there's a message in this," he says. "She didn't hesitate to help. If this animal that's supposed to be below us can be this way, why can't we?"[7]

The assumption that animals exist only to survive and procreate, without any higher sensibility or purpose, makes for interesting scientific debate. Many biologists, ethologists, and comparative psychologists refuse to consider animal behavior as anything other than an assortment of conditioned and reflexive behaviors, and firmly resist using the language of morality, or making anthropomorphic judgments, when discussing animal behavior. Our scientific tradition reflects an unfortunate assumption that evolution of the species and survival of the fittest lead only to unrestricted competition and the pursuit of self-interests. From this point of view, every nonhuman creature is incapable of compassion, caring, or generosity, other than toward its immediate kin—behaviors presumably driven by instincts to protect progeny and their own participation in the gene pool. This is a narrow interpretation of Charles Darwin (who himself did not hesitate to speculate about emotions in animals), and it denies that animals experience any emotions at all. But if you were to ask people who train animals, or those who have pets, whether or not animals experience and exhibit kindness or compassion, there wouldn't be much of a controversy. Animals express ordinary grace in the most extraordinary ways, and we have constant evidence of this.

The question raised by the story of Binti is whether or not there is any beauty in the beast. The question is important because understanding animal behavior can give us insight into our own human animal nature. For although we put great store in the idea that human intelligence and reason are what separate us from all other species, the fact is that the lower centers of our brains are shared by all vertebrates, and more than 98 percent of our DNA sequences correspond with those of chimpanzees.[8] From a biological perspective, there is a connection between human behavior and that of other animals, particularly primates.

Japanese scientists have conducted experiments to discover whether or not animals naturally express empathy. Their subjects were thirty-four young chimpanzees who were observed as they responded to a feigned injury by the experimenter. In the experimental group, the researcher pretended to injure her index finger and expressed pain verbally and through facial expressions. In the control group, the researcher smiled and waved her hand to the chimpanzee. There was a significantly different response when the researcher appeared to have been hurt. The chimpanzees continued to gaze at the injured hand far longer than they did when the experimenter was simply waving. These researchers concluded that such different behaviors indicated a basis for empathetic behavior in chimpanzees similar to that seen in human babies.[9]

Robert Yerkes, an early researcher of primate behavior, worked at a time (the 1920s) when any suggestion of emotion in animals was thoroughly ridiculed by the scientific community, and yet he, too, observed chimpanzees' thoughtfulness in caring for an injured companion. One little female was so sick that she could do nothing more than lie on the floor. Yerkes noted that even during their normal boisterous play, the other animals carefully avoided disturbing her. Occasionally one of the others would go over to her, touch her gently, and caress her. Yerkes was perfectly sure about what he saw: "A certain solicitude, sympathy, and pity, as well as almost human expression of consideration were thus manifested by these little creatures."[10]

More contemporary observations have shown that chimpanzees and other primates, such as macaques, clean each other's wounds, wave flies away from injured companions, protect the injured from danger, and travel more slowly if the wounded cannot keep up. These demonstrations of sympathy and caretaking are not restricted to primates. Similar behavior has been observed among dolphins, elephants, lemurs, and other species. What is most difficult for researchers to communicate, in scientific language, are the nuances of expression that they observe in these animals. Ethologist and zoologist Frans de Waal understands that animal behavior is often interpreted in simplistic terms because the researcher is determined to avoid the attribution of any feelings or consciousness. Yet his own observations confirm what other scientists, such as Yerkes, have seen. In his book *Good-Natured*, he writes, "I believe there is more to the cleaning of wounds; many hard-to-convey details in the behavior of chimpanzees (the way they approach an injured individual; the concerned look in their eyes; the care they take not to hurt) that make me intuitively agree with the views of Yerkes."[11]

De Waal has documented many examples of animal grace. He writes: "Animals, particularly those close to us, show an enormous spectrum of emotions and different kinds of relationships. It is only fair to reflect this fact in a broad array of terms. If animals can have enemies they can have friends; if they can cheat they can be honest; if they can be spiteful they can also be kind and altruistic. Semantic distinctions between animal and human behavior often obscure fundamental similarities; a discussion of morality will be pointless if we allow our language to be distorted by a denial of benign motives and emotions in animals."[12]

When my yellow Labrador, Dorothy, was less than a year old, she was hit by a car. We rushed her to the vet, who saved not only her leg but also her life. He said that she was very lucky; had she been a half-second slower she undoubtedly would have had massive internal injuries. As it was, her back right leg was shattered. Because she was young and her bones were still forming, the prognosis was good, but it was important for her to stay very quiet for a few weeks. We had to keep her separated from her dog friends, whose constant desire to jump and play with her might threaten her rehabilitation.

During her recovery, Dorothy and I spent time at my friend Margaret's house in Nag's Head, North Carolina. Dorothy stayed in one bedroom on a big, flat pillow on the floor, and we set up a baby-gate so that she could see and hear us but wouldn't be able to rough-house with other dogs. Another friend, Wendy, was there for the weekend with her golden retriever, Austin, a two-year-old male. Austin took an immediate and intense liking to Dorothy. He would sit at the baby-gate, whining and howling, until she pulled herself over to him. Their faces would meet between the spaces in the gate, and they would fall asleep with their noses touching. As Dorothy continued to heal, we were able to let her lie in the room with the other dogs. Austin would sit behind Dorothy, put his paws on either side of her injured leg, and growl if the other dogs came too near. Then he would fall asleep with his head in the air, hovering over her leg. What was most amazing to all of us was that this attention didn't appear to be sexual in any way, but instead was protective, as a father dog might act toward his pup. As we watched the whole scenario unfold, my friends and I had no doubt that Austin's behavior arose from friendship and caring.

Despite the philosophical and theological debates about whether or not goodness is part of human nature, and all the scientific arguments about compassion and empathy in animals, the truest revelations about human nature come from looking at actual behavior. It can be argued that if we're ever going to get to the bottom of human motivation—to whether we act from innate or learned goodness—we need to look at the earliest examples of our own behavior: to the child in his mother's arms; to the infant next to her sibling in the crib. What many researchers have found is that compassion, empathy, and love are natural to children and are evident at the very start of life.

Developmental psychologist Martin Hoffman of New York University has demonstrated clearly that newborns, even in the first day of their lives, show remarkable empathy and respond to other infants' crying by beginning to cry themselves. Studies have shown that this crying response is more immediate and more intense than an infant's reaction to other noises, including computer-simulated crying. It is hard to imagine that this natural empathy has been instructed or taught through cultural experience—after all, these infants are only one day old. Instead, these observations strongly suggest that there is a biological predisposition toward empathy in human beings,[13] which makes a great deal of sense when you consider that our species is a social one. Few early hominids would have survived had they not learned to cooperate; to hunt together and to protect each other from predators and other dangers. The importance of cooperation and sharing in societies that continue to live as hunter-gatherers today is obvious, for the success of hunting with primitive weapons depends on organization and firm reliance on each group member playing a role. From a sociobiological point of view, there is a considerable advantage to being able to empathize; to recognize the moods and intentions of other members of the species during cooperative activities. It helps to know how others are feeling.

Neurological research into the biology of empathy has shown that it is regulated by a part of the brain called the amygdala, a small almond-shaped cluster of interconnected structures located just above the most ancient part of the human brain, the brainstem. This structure plays a key role in the organization of appropriate emotional reactions. Leslie Brothers, a psychiatrist investigating the neurophysiology of emotions, aptly sums up the importance of empathy for nonhuman primates: "The survival value of such a system is obvious. The perception of another individual's approach should give rise to a specific pattern of physiological response—and very quickly—tailored to whether the intent is to bite, to have a quiet grooming session, or to copulate."[14]

Other research has shown that one-year-old children are perfectly capable of expressing concern for and offering comfort to family members who are hurt. In a series of experiments conducted in the subjects' homes, psychologists Carolyn Zahn-Waxler, Marian Radke-Yarrow, and their colleagues at the National Institute of Mental Health instructed family members of young children to feign sadness by sobbing, pain by yelling "ouch," and distress by coughing or choking. The children responded to each of these stimuli by patting and hugging the sufferer or by rubbing the "hurt" spot. While these subjects' reactions were strongest when they were interacting with their mothers, they also exhibited empathy toward complete strangers.[15]

Although a child's instinct to act compassionately is there from the start, behavioral science has also shown that the influence of the outer world on the development of personality and other aspects of our humanity is enormous, and that parents and peers have great power to shape a child's view of the world. While this has always been understood intuitively, research into the exquisite dance between nature and nurture that shapes human beings is providing fascinating evidence about how it happens. Human infants are not born tabulae rasae—blank slates—but are endowed with instincts and archetypal expectations about life. Current studies from neurobiologists show that the brain begins working long before it is finished developing. Even in utero, ten to twelve weeks after conception, the human brain begins to lay down a network of connections through repeated and coordinated bursts of neural activity. A baby is born with a brain that contains more than one hundred billion nerve cells, and a trillion glial cells that protect and nourish these neurons. At this stage of development, it is as if all the wiring is completed but the specific connections that will be used are still to be determined by later sensory experience. Neurobiologist Carla Shatz of the University of California, Berkeley, observes, "What the brain has done is lay out circuits that are its best guess about what's required for vision, for language, for whatever."

Trillions of connections between neurons, more than could ever be used, are created. Then, in a sort of "use it or lose it" process, the brain begins to eliminate those connections that are seldom or never used, based upon that infant's experience. For example, research has shown that children who are rarely touched or have few opportunities for playful interaction develop brains that are 20 to 30 percent smaller than normal for their age. On the other hand, loving, rich, and stimulating experiences produce brains with vibrant and multiple connections between nerve cells. And while learning can take place throughout the lifespan, by the age of ten, the brain begins to relentlessly destroy its weakest neural connections. By adolescence, around the age of eighteen, the brain loses a great deal of its plasticity but increases in other powers. Thus, while a person can change throughout life, what a child learns early in life becomes increasingly difficult to change as he or she grows older.[16]

Recently, I read an article about infant twins. They were several months premature, with very low birth weights. The older twin was almost three-quarters of a pound heavier and had far more vigorous pulmonary and cardiovascular functioning. The younger twin was being cared for around the clock, and the prognosis for her survival was poor. The two of them were kept in separate incubators until a wise and compassionate neonatal nurse suggested that the sicker twin might benefit from contact with her sibling, since they had spent five months together in their mother's womb. The infants were moved to a new incubator that could accommodate both of them. As soon as they were put together, the older, more robust twin put her arm over her sister, pulled her close, and fell asleep. The sick twin soon began to show significant increases in heart and lung function. Within four weeks, both were discharged from the hospital. The photograph that accompanied the article showed the twins nestled together and smiling.

Sociologists Jane Piliavin and Hong-Wen Charng, in their review of the literature on altruism, conclude that altruistic intention and behavior exist very early in life and are part of what it means to be a human being. Citing both theoretical and empirical studies from social science literature, they confirm what most parents of young children already know. "There appears to be a 'paradigm shift' away from the earlier position that behavior that appears to be altruistic must, under closer scrutiny, be revealed as reflecting egoistic motives," they write. "Rather, theory and data now being advanced are more compatible with the view that true altruism—acting with the goal of benefiting another—does exist and is a part of human nature."[17]

Much in the way that infants, being closer to pure human nature, give us clues to our natural drives and instincts, human societies that live close to the natural world can teach us a great deal about what is intrinsic to our species. For example, the Hodi (pronounced ho-day) people of south-central Venezuela live today much as their ancestors have for centuries. They are a nomadic people who travel through the mountains between the Orinoco and Amazon river basins. Robert Storrie, a British anthropologist who is studying this tribal culture, points out that the name Hodi means "all of you like me." Sharing and generosity are part of their value system. These people hunt, fish, grow maize and rice, and gather wild vegetables and fruit together. When a hunt is successful, the meat is distributed equally to all in the community. "There is no reason to be competitive with each other," Storrie points out, "because they share everything. The Hodi consider not being generous a crime, much like stealing." There is very little conflict or aggression in Hodi society. Villages are arranged with several families living under the same thatched roof. If one member of the tribe has a problem with another, he or she simply sleeps in another dwelling until the issue is resolved or forgotten.[18]

We see similar behaviors—sharing, welcoming, and inclusion—in many indigenous societies. Among Native American tribes, for example, there are often words, salutations, and chants that reflect benevolence and connection with others. The Lakota Sioux look toward Father Sky and declare: *"Mitakuye oyasin"*— "We are all one people."

A strong case can be made for the idea that a great deal of human nature is good and is consistent with values such as compassion, fairness, generosity, and inclusion. Zoologist Desmond Morris concurs, and captures the evolutionary significance of this idea for our species by noting, "It has often been said that 'the law forbids men to do only what their instincts incline them to do.' If this is true, then the human animal must by nature be a cheating, thieving, torturing rapist. But I think not. The image of the primeval brute beating his companions over the head with a large club and dragging his female off to a cave by her hair is a cartoonist's fiction. There is no way in which we could have successfully evolved as an actively cooperative hunting species if we had lived like that. To have thrived as we must have done in those early days, to spread all over the globe, we must have been biologically a remarkably peaceful, restrained and helpful animal."[19]

In light of what we see in the world as part of our everyday reality, it may be difficult to recognize humanity's common source and our common destinies. The belief in the fundamental evil of human nature makes it much more difficult to understand "ordinary grace," and leaves us without an explanation for why those who have not been taught—or forced—to behave according to moral principles and values would choose to do good.

Imagine how our views about ourselves and others might change if we believed that we were all born with the innate capacity for goodness as well as for evil. What would the world be like if we cherished the idea that each human being, indeed every living thing, is a reflection and a manifestation of the love of a benevolent creator? Would we treat each other and the earth differently, more compassionately? Would we all encounter and express more ordinary grace if we believed that each of us were an embodiment of the divine and surrounded by God's love?

To believe that human beings have *innate* goodness requires that we undergo a paradigm shift, a dramatic change in our culture's core values and beliefs. This shift allows us to see that each and every one of us is born, not with original sin, but with all the potential to be fully human. Lessons from the natural world should convince us that we are part of God's great plan, part of nature itself: we are *born* with the capacity to express goodness and grace. Episcopal priest and scholar Matthew Fox calls this capacity for ordinary grace "original blessing," which he describes as essential grace, a gift given to us by a loving creator who invites us to participate fully in life and to stay close to the natural world, singing the praises of existence itself.[20] The Dalai Lama says that we are born "originally pure," and that human nature is basically gentle and kind.[21] It is the truth behind what fifteenth-century mystic Julian of Norwich said: "We have been loved since before the beginning."[22]

What we choose to believe not only changes our perception of the world; it changes us as well. Would it not be cynical to believe that one little girl protected her brother from traffic and another gave her gift away solely out of self-interest or because of a system of rewards and punishments? Why shouldn't we see those acts as arising from innate goodness, rather than from discipline and control? Psychologist William Eckhardt, who devoted many years of research to the study of compassion, once observed that he had never encountered a compassionate adult who did not have "radical trust in human nature." He wrote, "Compassion is a function of faith in human nature, while compulsion is a function of lack of faith in human nature (the belief that man is basically evil)."[23] Among the people I have interviewed and studied, there is a clear understanding that goodness resides in every human being, no matter how difficult it may be to see.

As we examine expressions of ordinary grace, we find ourselves thinking more and more in terms of the larger scheme of things, for a transcendent perspective is required in order to fully appreciate the beauty of human beings and our relationship to the divine. Those who exhibit such grace have not forgotten what we are here for, and that our destiny is in our own hands. They remember what many of us have overlooked and what was echoed in the haunting words of poet and novelist G. K. Chesterton at the beginning of this century: "Among all the strange things that men have forgotten, the most universal and catastrophic lapse of memory is that by which they have forgotten that they are living on a star."[24]

3.

Angels

If a person were in rapture as great as St. Paul once experienced

and learned that a neighbor were in need of a cup of soup,

it would be best to withdraw from his rapture

and give the person the soup she needs.

—Meister Eckhart

Just thirty miles from the pristine golf courses and resorts of Phoenix live people who have been described as the "poorest of the poor." The Gila River Indian Reservation is home to more than nine thousand Native American people of the Pima, Maricopa, Papago, Navaho, and (predominantly) Apache tribes. In spite of the two profitable Native American–owned casinos that employ about a thousand people, almost everyone here lives in squalor. Some work for barely a living wage as farmhands, but most, having searched unsuccessfully for work nearby, are stranded without any means of transportation, public or otherwise, to get to other places of employment. Therefore, most families subsist on an average of fifty dollars a month, eat a meager diet of bread and refried beans, and live in dilapidated one-room, mud-roofed shacks without plumbing or electricity. Burlap or plastic drop-cloths cover the window frames but offer no protection from the cold winds of the Arizona desert that sweep through the houses at night. Despite their great poverty and despair, these people's lives are made a bit better by the great heart of a seventy-two-year-old woman.

Fourteen years ago, Florence "Flo" Denomme was diagnosed with a very serious form of breast cancer. "I thought I was a goner," she says in halting speech. "I prayed day in and day out. I was Catholic all my life—I went to church, but I didn't know there was a God up there all the time." After radical surgery, chemotherapy, and radiation, her breast cancer was cured, and she knew that God had spared her for some purpose. Since that time Flo has dedicated her life, quietly and on her own, to easing the pain of her poverty-stricken neighbors in Guadalupe, South Phoenix, Chandler, and the Gila River Indian Reservation.

Flo rises at four-thirty every morning and begins to cook, sort the many clothes and household items that she has collected for donations, and set up her schedule for the day. After these chores, she takes a short break to attend mass, stops at the store to pick up milk and meat, and then drives across the desert where she will go from house to house with food and supplies. She returns home at five or six, makes dinner for her husband and herself, then begins to write out her tentative schedule for the next day. This is a full-time job for Flo, but she knows that she must do it. "The people I work with are worse than poor," she says. "Even a dog lives better than they do. Some get a very, very small pension. I want to know why the people are not living any better with those casinos there. I've tried to talk to the managers but no one gives me any answers."

Weekday and weekend, rain or shine, and in the blazing Arizona summer heat, Flo makes her deliveries. She doesn't consider taking a day off. "People never stop needing food, so why should I stop delivering?" she asks.

Flo was born and raised in Rhode Island, where she met and married her husband, Jerry. He suffered from asthma and their oldest son from bronchitis, and they were told that the symptoms might improve in the warm, arid climate of the Southwest. They moved to Arizona. "It seemed like they were always at the doctor's, and we decided to try it," she tells me. That was forty-one years ago, and their health did improve. Today, the whole family helps Flo with her work. Using their own funds and whatever money they can raise through donations, they have built houses for families on the reservation who were living in shacks. They build simple, unadorned houses, but with windows and doors that close, indoor plumbing, and small kitchens. "The people can't even afford a fifty-dollar-a-month house payment. What we build is not fancy but it has a bathroom, a kitchen, a bedroom, a roof, and electricity. The people have never had a bathroom in their house before, they used a little hut outside. It's not much to live in, but if you could only see their faces when they move into it."

Flo's generosity and tireless work haven't gone unnoticed. This senior citizen, who has a debilitating form of palsy, simply says that she cannot stand by and do nothing. One day in the fall of 1994, a reporter from a local television station called and asked to interview her. She didn't want to do it, but the reporter was persistent: "Flo, I want to go out with you and see what you do. People that don't have the handicap that you do are not doing anything. It can show other people with handicaps that they can do something too." Flo reluctantly agreed to be interviewed, in the hope that her story might encourage other people, especially those with disabilities, to get involved. "I didn't want to be embarrassed. I was so shaky, it was like putting quarters in a vibrating bed," she says. "I turned to that reporter and said 'Look what you made me go through.' "

But the publicity that Flo so resisted did touch the hearts of others. People began to call and ask how they could help. On Thanksgiving and Christmas, many volunteers helped Flo cook for more than four hundred people. They prepared a feast with chicken, ham, vegetables, and desserts. Two years ago, Flo and this group of volunteers started a nonprofit foundation to support Flo's tireless efforts to make a difference in the lives of the less fortunate people of her community. In addition to collecting and helping Flo deliver food (she still does all the daily cooking herself), the group has established scholarships and furnished materials and volunteers to build the same kind of simple houses that Flo and Jerry had built by themselves. There are no paid staff, and all funds and donations are used directly to help the poor.

Flo doesn't like the name of the group. With her typical humility, she wanted to call it "To Other People." But the board, composed of ordinary men and women (retired executives, a free-lance writer, an engineer, a customer service representative, and a small-business owner), told her they wanted to name it after her. "No," she said, "I don't want my name on it." One of the board members told her that they wanted to use her name so that people would remember her and carry on her work after she was no longer able to do it. She still resisted, and then the board threatened to quit, so they compromised, adding a w to "Flo" and calling it the Flow from the Heart Foundation. Today, hundreds of volunteers generously give of their time and energy to help the people Flo Denomme could not pass by.[1]

Flo's palsy is incurable and causes her to shake all the time. Her speech is faltering and she tells me that she wishes she could speak better, but what she is saying more than makes up for her lack of fluidity. She has four children, four grandchildren, and a great-grandchild; she would have a full life without working every day to help the poor. She's so busy that last year she couldn't get her Christmas shopping done for her own family, but that doesn't matter, she says. Both she and her husband are retired, and they are not wealthy people, but they share what they have. Sometimes they use their own money to pay electric or water bills for a reservation family, as well as buy food and building supplies to fix up houses. She continually discovers new families who need help and adds them to her burgeoning delivery list. Twice each week Flo fasts on nothing but water, to keep herself in touch with what hunger feels like and offering it up to God. "There are so many people to help and so many people to thank," she says. "Last year we collected three hundred blankets. It still wasn't enough—the nights are so cold. At home we have two blankets on our bed, the heat on, and it's still cold. If we are cold, then they are freezing. I sometimes get tired but when you see those little children with their runny noses you know that you can't stop. God blessed me and saved my life to do this work. My life was spared and I certainly won't sit home and feel sorry for myself. I knew that He had something else for me to do. It's in my blood for me to do what I'm doing. Those people need me and I need them. It's like I have an angel on my shoulder."

Like Florence Denomme, Maria Santos understands the importance of compassion as an action. She would live a full life even without a ministry prompted by the Holy Spirit. This forty-eight-year-old Portuguese immigrant and mother of four is celebrating her twentieth anniversary with her husband Frank, a career Navy man. Three of their children still live at home, and that includes two teenagers who, Maria claims, "can drive me crazy." She holds a part-time job as a phone counselor for the Christian Broadcast Network, is active in her evangelical Christian church, and cleans houses to earn extra money. It is easy to wonder why, with as jam-packed a schedule as hers, she spends hours each day baking bread and preparing soup and stew for homeless people in her city. She says that this is part of the mission of her life—to express compassion as well as she can. She is a vibrant woman who laughs easily and moves her hands grace-fully, as if she intends to pull the correct English word out of thin air. She could be any average middle-aged housewife in Virginia Beach. But, she says, she serves as a vessel for God's will and cannot imagine her life without this work.

In April 1994, Maria was on her way to an English class for non-native speakers. She says she has considerable problems with English, especially the verbs, and it was time to do something about that. On the second day of her class she decided to park her car behind the school building because the rear entrance was much closer to her classroom. As she stepped out of her car, she saw a dirty-looking old man curled up on the pavement between two large air conditioners behind a convenience store. Although it was early in the spring, the day was very hot and muggy. The old man looked frail, perhaps ill, and she thought, "Oh my Lord, that old man will die in this heat." Then she heard a voice inside her head. She is certain that it was the voice of the Holy Spirit. This had never happened before in her life, but she was quite sure of who was speaking to her. The voice said, "Go and speak to that man." Maria was scared. She had never spoken to anyone like this man before. In fact, she had never directly encountered a homeless person. She lives in a well-tended middle-class suburb where the homeless are mostly invisible. "We speak of them but we don't see them if we don't look for them," she says.

She resisted the voice that again insisted that she speak to the old man. But, because the inner voice was so commanding, she approached the man in spite of her fear. "Woman, what are you doing?" he said. "Don't you know you're not supposed to talk to strangers?" "Yes," she answered, "but the Holy Spirit is in my ear, and I'm told that I should talk to you."

"Ah," the old man replied, "so you know the Lord?"

Maria said that she did know the Lord. He had healed her many years before during a particularly difficult time of her life. The old man asked if she knew the Bible passages of John 3:16 and Matthew 7:21. She was familiar with John—"For God so loved the world that he gave his only Son, so that everyone who believes in him may not perish but may have eternal life." She did not remember the verse from Matthew, so the old man recited it for her: "Not everyone who says to me, 'Lord, Lord,' will enter the kingdom of heaven but only the one who does the will of my Father in heaven."

The man started to tell her about the Bible. Maria said to him, "Oh, you are just a little sheep that got lost here." The old man replied that he was homeless; that he lived between the air conditioning units. She could see mounds of newspaper and cardboard that he had used to create padding for the ground and something like a roof. He told her that he slept there year-round. In the winter he felt some heat from the air conditioners, and they created a slight breeze on hot summer days. Maria told him that she would return after her class.

She related the story to her teacher and classmates, who sternly warned her about speaking to men like this one. "Never talk to them. They're dangerous," she was told. Her teacher and classmates reignited her original fear, but she had promised the man that she would return, and at the end of her class she went back to the rear of the convenience store. She bought the old man a bottle of soda, but was frightened again when he began to clutch his stomach and yelp in pain. They knelt together on the ground and she prayed with him that his pain would pass, and within a few minutes he said, "I feel better now."

"I have to go and clean a house. But I'll come back later and I'll bring some food to you," she told him.

She and her son Michael worked quickly to finish the house-cleaning; then she returned to her home and baked two extra loaves of the round Portuguese bread that she makes each day for her family. She peeled potatoes, carrots, other vegetables, and made a stew thick with beans and pasta. By the time she was ready to deliver the food to the old man, it was dark. She took her son with her, but they were both afraid to drive behind the convenience store and look for the old man. She didn't see him at first, but Michael pointed him out in a dark corner behind the building. He was with another, younger man. "I was very scared because now there were two men there. But I get out of my car and say 'Sir, are you okay? You want me to bring you this food?'" The old man smiled and said to the other guy, "You see, I told you she's coming." And then he knelt and said, "Please pray for me. I felt better when you prayed for me." And they sat on the ground and she prayed for the old man. When they were finished, the younger man asked that they pray for him too. "He was very beautiful: blue eyes, long blond hair—but his clothes were very, very dirty," Maria remembers. They prayed for him, and then she said, "You want more than prayer, you want the Lord in your life. You don't have to tell me your life, you don't have to tell me what bothers you, but you can confess to the Lord your sins. You tell him, whatever you want from him, he's going to do it for you."

The younger man began to cry and asked the Lord to take his alcohol problems away from him. He wanted to be delivered, Maria says, and so she put her hands on him and prayed for him. "Where can I go to be baptized?" he asked. Maria told him to go to the Open Door Chapel, which was close by. "I was still too scared to bring somebody with me, you know," she says. The younger man left, and then the old man started to cry in pain and clutch his stomach. Maria told her son that they must get him to a hospital, so they lifted him up and laid him in the back-seat of their car. They drove to a nearby hospital and waited for several hours after the old man had been taken into an examining room. Maria asked a nurse about him but was told that because she was not a relative the hospital couldn't give her any information.

The next day Maria worked and then went back to the hospital, but still she was given no information. She drove to the back of the convenience store but the old man was not there. That evening, Maria was cooking for friends who were coming for dinner, when she again heard the voice of the Holy Spirit. "You fear the ones that are hungry. But there are many people who are hungry," it said. She told her husband that she was going to deliver some food in case the old man or others were there behind the convenience store. She drove everywhere around the area but couldn't find anyone who appeared to be homeless or hungry. "Lord, why can't I find him? I'm following the voice as you tell me to but still I can't find him."

As she passed the Department of Social Services building she saw one man sitting on a bench and, at first, thought it might be the old man. She drove up and rolled down her window. "I'm scared to talk to another guy again, but I said, 'Sir, have you seen an old man here? I brought him Thursday night to the hospital. He said he was homeless. And now I'm bringing some bread and I can't find him,' " Maria recalls. The man said, "I don't know him but I'm homeless and I could sure use some of your bread."

She parked her car and gave the man some bread. As they were talking, seven more men came out of the woods behind the building, and she shared the bread with all of them. One man told her that he had been drinking alcohol all of his life and that the Lord didn't love him anymore. "No, it's not true," she said, "the Lord loves you so much."

Every day since then she has gone to pray with the homeless and bring them her gifts of Portuguese bread and homemade soup. Her son has built a small greenhouse in their backyard, where she now grows vegetables and herbs for these meals. Two fat brown chickens provide eggs for the bread. It is, she says, "like a love connection," and she is certain that the old man was an angel sent to help her understand her mission in this life.

Maria has created a ministry called Love and Caring for the

Homeless, Inc. She organized fund-raising efforts that have allowed her to purchase two small clapboard houses (one for women and one for men) where homeless people who seek a better life can live. These two houses are the beginning of a mission to provide warm havens where homeless people can begin the long journey of realizing the Lord's love for them, establishing self-esteem, finding jobs, and saving money so that they can move into their own apartments. One day, while Maria was cleaning a bathroom at her part-time job, she had a vision of ten such houses.

"The Lord showed me ten little houses that have doors that are rounded at the top. I'm cleaning Lilly's house when that happened, and cleaning the bathroom floor with a brush when the Lord spoke to me. I said, 'Lord, about that dream?' But I knew it wasn't a dream because I was awake. And he spoke again and said, 'Ten houses.' I said, 'Lord, how much is it going to be for ten houses? That's going to be a lot of money.' I'm sure the Holy Spirit got mad at me because I couldn't hear no more. But I knew that I had started already a house for children in Portugal and I thought, 'Oh my God, everyone there gave me that house. One gave me the floors, another helped me build it, one gave me cement, another one gave the bricks.' I said, 'O Lord, forgive me. I forgot.' "

As people in the community learned of Maria's ministry, they began to contribute money and help. But there were so many problems in bringing these safe houses to reality that she found herself questioning her faith from time to time. Some days she would return home crying and wondering how she was ever going to accomplish all that was being asked of her. "Look, I'm waiting for three months to find that house and it's problems after problems after problems and I said, 'Lord I know you gave me this faith. I'm not going to go back even when people say no.' " Maria is aware that some people might think she is a little crazy to believe that the Holy Spirit speaks to her or to devote so much of her time and energy to what appears to be such an insurmountable problem. Nevertheless, she continues to bake her bread and pray for the people who need it.

"Sometimes the Lord can say no. Look at the first houses we tried to buy. We really believed that those were the houses and we go for three contracts and pray and go there and anoint those houses and God said no. You see, He had something better. The Lord knew we were going to have a lot of problems with the neighbors over there, because they had already called and said, 'You're not going to bring those people over here, are you?' They don't understand that these people are people just like you and me. As soon as they get Jesus in their hearts they change. As soon as they have a room, they're not homeless no more. They're just like you and me. They're homeless now because they don't have an address. We thank God for these houses because now they will have an address. God provides for us. Thank you, Lord."

Kathy Simmons heard no voice of the Holy Spirit when she decided that there were too many hungry people in her community. She drives a trolley in Pensacola, Florida, and her route takes her past homeless people sleeping on the sidewalks and benches in the park.

"These people out here, out of their luck, all they need is someone to show them they care. Be a friend to them. Treat them like anybody else. Don't treat 'em no different," she says.

Every morning this forty-five-year-old woman gets up early and makes sandwiches with tuna fish, egg salad, or bologna and cheese. When her budget allows it, she buys turkey—but she is careful to never make the same sandwich two days in a row. In the sweetest projection I have ever heard, with an utterly compassionate sentiment that shows no distinction between the giver and the recipient, she says, "I don't like that, so I figured they wouldn't."

During her run she gives excellent tours of the city, and whenever she passes those in need she drops off her sandwiches and packages of snack cakes to them. She remembers one homeless man, dirty and disheveled, who got on her trolley. She was a little afraid of him because of the way he looked, but nevertheless she put a handful of her own quarters in the slot so that he could ride. They talked for an hour, in between her tour announcements. Two weeks later she saw this man again. He was clean-shaven and neatly dressed, going to detox, and trying to find a part-time job. John Allman of the Pensacola *News Journal* reported this story and commented on the profound impact that Kathy Simmons's compassion had had on him when he rode on the trolley with her. "Her human kindness outshined the history around me," he wrote, "as I listened and learned and looked at my city through different eyes."[2]

The impact of Kathy Simmons's compassion on the decision of this homeless man to seek a new life is not surprising. Like Florence Denomme and Maria Santos, she has discovered that her caring for others has the power not only to improve their circumstances but to change them as people. It is what Aesop taught more than twenty-five hundred years ago. "No act of kindness, no matter how small, is ever wasted," he wrote. Trappist monk Thomas Merton commented eloquently in his many journals about the importance of love and compassion and their transforming power. Like the metamorphosis of a caterpillar into a butterfly, compassion becomes an act of co-creation with the divine. "How can one tell how much he owes to the goodness of those who love him?" he wrote. "If we knew what people in their love for us do to save us from damnation by the simple fact of their friendship for us, we would learn some humility."[3]

4.

No Greater Gift

You are so weak. Give up to grace.

The ocean takes care of each wave 'til it gets to shore.

You need more help than you know.[1]

—Jelaluddin Rumi

I was running late, and had less than an hour to drive to the grocery store, get through the salad bar, eat my lunch, return phone calls, and write up the morning's notes for work. I got into the express checkout line, money in hand, my eyes glued to the big wall clock by the supermarket's doors—forty-eight minutes now until my next appointment.

The older woman in front of me was unloading her cart very slowly, far too sluggishly for me. I could feel myself becoming tight, stressed, and cranky. In spite of my great commitment to working on my own spiritual growth and my deep faith in the presence of grace, I was feeling particularly peevish on that afternoon. I'm ashamed to admit that I was so focused on all of the "important things" I had to be doing that day that all I could think was "Hurry up, I don't have time for this." I found myself looking into her basket and hoping she had violated the ten-items-or-less rule, enforced in express lines throughout the world, and clearly proclaimed on the large sign over our heads. If that were the case, I could give her a subtle dirty look, the kind I've gotten when I've pushed the limit and convinced myself that two containers of yogurt really counted as only one item, since they were, after all, the same flavor.

Just at that moment I realized that she was buying many cans of Ensure, a nutritional supplement. This was the same product that my family had purchased by the caseload when my mother was dying, in the last stages of leukemia, and had no appetite. We had tried everything to get her to eat: tiny portions of her favorite foods arranged artfully on a small plate and served at any hour of the day or night when she might be hungry; importing her favorite Italian lemon ice from New Jersey; and, as a last resort, sneaking this particular supplement into malted milks and ice cream sodas. She said it tasted like "metal," and could invariably tell when we had slipped it in. Despite the television ads that show healthy, older people able to scuba dive and hike up mountains because they include this product in their diet, I believe that people really buy it because someone in their household isn't eating very well because of being sick—usually very sick.

When the woman had finished unloading her cart, she turned

toward me. We looked at each other and I could see sadness in her eyes. I felt a rush of empathy for her and my eyes welled up with tears. In less than a second my feelings for this woman were profoundly changed. No longer irritable and in a hurry, I could feel her pain; I knew it very well because I had been there. Instead of hurrying her along, I felt like asking if there was anything I could do to help her. I was experiencing what Tibetan Buddhists call *tonglen*—"giving and receiving." It is this energy that opens a person to the truth of the suffering in others. My own broken heart opened a way for this woman's pain to enter, and I was transformed from a person running late and feeling testy into someone who understood, if only for this moment, the amazing relationship between us. Her expression told me that she knew it too. We transcended the false belief that we are all separate and unrelated beings. The woman smiled and nodded and, without a word, communicated the deepest feeling of connection. It was a moment of simple and ineffable communion, the presence of grace in a checkout line.

This is the way that we're *supposed* to relate to each other all the time, and it is what is possible when we allow ourselves to move beyond the quotidian and to open ourselves up to the always-present grace. Vietnamese Buddhist monk and Nobel Peace Prize nominee Thich Nhat Hanh has called this openness "interbeing," and describes it as the intrinsic "inter-is" that characterizes everything in the universe. "When we see the nature of interbeing," he writes, "barriers between ourselves and others are dissolved, and peace, love, and understanding are possible.

Whenever there is understanding, compassion is born."[2] This is what Jesus meant when he said, "Love your brother like your soul."[3] Jewish tradition proclaims that the truth of *shekinah*, the Presence of God, is found throughout creation; the mystical Kabbalah reflects on this essential oneness of reality: "The entire chain is one. Down to the last link, everything is linked with everything else; so divine essence is below as well as above, in heaven and on earth. There is nothing else."[4] The belief that all beings are part of a connected cosmic web, all sparks from the same original fireball, is informed not only by modern research in physics, bioecology, chemistry, and chaos theory, but by every great religion and tradition of wisdom known to the world.

But many of us have forgotten our own true natures and the exquisite unity that binds all things together. Our modern world, with its emphasis on materialism, rationalism, and separatism, has lost sight of the cosmos as a coherent whole in which every aspect of creation is vitally related to everything else, and in which each of us is an indispensable part of all that is.

These next stories touch my soul each time I think about them. To me, they illuminate the exquisite interrelationship that is possible between people. They relate directly to the intricate web of connectedness that washes over and through us.

On any given day, more than 51,000 Americans are on the national waiting list for organ donation. Only 19,000 of them are likely to receive organs, and most of the others will die before a donor can be found. Most people are surprised to learn that the human body contains more than twenty-five organs and tissues that can give the gift of life to another person. Almost every death contains opportunities for life, and while an increasing number of people make provisions for their organs to be donated when they die—about fifty percent of white Americans and about one-third of African-Americans and Hispanics—only one-third of these organs are ever actually harvested. Thirty percent of families override their loved ones' decisions and refuse to give the organs. Most distressingly, another thirty percent of families are *never asked* about organ donations by doctors and medical personnel because it is a hard thing to ask a bereaved family. What a difficult, chilling decision it must be for families to make the choice to donate a loved one's organs at the time of his or her death. But every day, families make such choices and save the lives of strangers in the process.

A phone ringing in the middle of the night can be a parent's worst nightmare, as it was for Carol Sprinkel on June 20, 1995. At two-thirty in the morning, her son's girlfriend, Amanda, called to say that Steven had been in a serious automobile accident. He had suffered massive head injuries and had been transferred to the University of Virginia Medical Center from a small regional hospital.

In a panic, Carol and her husband Pierce drove the fifty miles to Charlottesville from their home in Elkton, Virginia. "Steven had had a previous car accident when he was a teenager and was brought to UVA, and on the way there, I had a sure feeling that he would be all right. I don't know if it's mother's intuition or what, but I didn't feel the same way this time," she recalls.

By the time Carol and Pierce arrived at the medical center, preliminary tests had indicated that Steven was brain-dead. He was still breathing, so the doctors decided to conduct further dye tests to make certain that no blood was going to his brain. Still, they asked Carol if she would be willing to sign papers to cut off life support. She refused until the results of the final test were in.

Family members were called, and they all rushed to Steven's side. Moments after the last one had arrived and told him how much he was loved, he stopped breathing. "It was like he couldn't go until he had a chance to be with everybody he loved," Carol told me. "But once we were all there, he went. We could see that his spirit was gone." The medical tests confirmed that Steven's brain was no longer functioning. He was dead.

Steven Cook was twenty-two years old and had been in excellent health. Carol was asked if she would consider donating his organs, and while the doctors understood that she needed time to grieve, there was only a small window of opportunity to remove his organs and deliver them to appropriate recipients if she agreed. She would have to make her decision immediately.

"I didn't know what to do," she said. "I looked at his driver's license and it was marked 'undecided' in the space where you declare whether you want to be an organ donor or not. But I felt that 'undecided' didn't mean no."

Carol had read articles and seen television programs that

explained the dire need for organs for transplants. She also knew that anti-rejection drugs and surgical techniques had progressed to the point at which organ recipients could be expected not only to survive longer but to live a far higher quality of life than before.

"I decided that donating Steven's organs was the only thing that could bring any good out of such a tragedy. In my heart, I knew that my decision could help other people. If the situation were the other way around, I would hope that there would be someone to help me or my family." In the midst of her agonizing grief and only moments after watching her son die, Carol consented and her son's organs were harvested.

At three-thirty in the afternoon of June 21, the University of Virginia Medical Center called Jim Brehony, my father, to tell him that a liver was available for transplant and that he had to come to Charlottesville immediately. My father was dying—and had been dying for at least six months—and this was his last hope for survival. Two years earlier he had started to get sick. At first, his doctor thought it was a problem with his gall bladder. They removed it, but he failed to improve. During a trip to Ohio he became so ill that he was rushed to an emergency room, where medical tests revealed that he was suffering from chronic active hepatitis C. The doctors believed that he had contracted it during a blood transfusion when he was eleven years old. For almost sixty years, the hepatitis virus had been slowly robbing his liver of its ability to function—and, since he'd shown no symptoms until recently, it had never been discovered. My father has always been blessed with good health. Even in his late sixties, he was more active than most people half his age—up at dawn every day for work. A great lover of life, he has many friends and enjoys a large variety of activities. He had nursed my mother through two terrible years prior to her death from leukemia, and when he started to get sick we thought it was a delayed reaction to all of the stress and grief he had experienced. After my mother died, he fell in love with a wonderful woman named Deanne whom he'd met during choir practice at his church. Falling in love with another woman was something he'd thought would never happen after forty-seven years of marriage to my mother, a woman he had dated since he was sixteen and had married as soon as he returned from the Second World War. Seeing this vibrant man become sicker and sicker was deeply painful for our whole family, and this was made worse because his illness began to show itself just months after we'd watched my mother slowly die.

As soon as our family heard news of the donor, we converged in Charlottesville. Like firefighters sliding down a pole into their waiting boots at the sound of the alarm, everyone was prepared, attached by a network of beepers and phone trees. The word went out that a miracle had happened. Dad had been given a chance to live. Even as they wheeled him down the hall to surgery he was typically upbeat and positive. In fact, he was joking with the nurses and seemed far calmer than the rest of us.

Everyone gathered in a waiting room hoping to get some sleep, but no one did. My stepmother Deanne and my stepsister

Shelley and her husband Dick sat quietly, nervously thumbing through magazines. My brother and sister-in-law, and my partner and I sat at a round table constructing a ten-thousand-piece jigsaw puzzle—anything to take our minds off our fears. After seven hours of staring at the puzzle, we had put three pieces together.

Following a grueling twelve-hour surgery, my father was recovering in an ICU and we were allowed to see him. It was a frightening sight. His face was so bloated and disfigured from the anesthesia that I thought he looked like Jabba the Hutt in *Star Wars*, though I didn't tell anyone that until much later. There were tubes fastened all over his body, and he was attached to at least eight different monitoring devices that were making clicking noises and flashing electronic numbers. He was clearly exhausted and disoriented and didn't recognize any of us, but he was alive. Dr. Stevenson, one of the transplant surgeons, told us that it was a most unusual surgery. Apparently, my father's liver had an anomaly in that the way the connecting vessels entered the organ was not "textbook" normal, and although this was not in itself a major problem, a longer surgery was usually required to make changes in how the blood vessels would attach to the new organ. When the donor liver was placed in my father's body, the doctors were shocked to see that it had *exactly* the same anomaly. The new liver fit perfectly.

The next day my father was transported to a regular hospital room, and by midday he was sitting in a chair holding court with the family. Six days later he was released from the hospital and sent home. At age sixty-nine, he had been given a second chance at life—what he now calls his "extra innings."

My whole extended family celebrated the good news. For the past year, prior to the operation, we had all worn little angel pins symbolizing our prayers and hopes that a liver would be found in time. At a family wedding, only a few weeks before the transplant, I had been moved to see all the men in their tuxedos wearing those little pins on their lapels. I decided that I would continue to wear my pin, no longer for my father, but now for the unknown person who had saved his life. At this time we knew only that his donor had been a man in his early twenties who had died after an automobile accident somewhere near Charlottesville. I prayed for him every night and gave thanks to his generous family for giving us such a blessed gift. I didn't like the idea of calling him "my father's liver donor"—it seemed too anonymous, too distant for somebody that felt this close—and, for reasons that I still do not understand, I began to pray for "Steven."

As soon as he returned home from the hospital, my father wrote a beautiful letter of thanks to his donor's family. He sent it to the transplant coordinator at the medical center, who assured him that it would be sent on to the family. He knew that his name and address would be removed from his letter, but also understood that the family could call the transplant coordinator to find out who he was and how to contact him if they chose to. He never heard from them, and we assumed that it would be too painful for them to revisit their son's death by getting in touch with him. My father continued to heal, and became actively involved in organ-donor education. He started to do volunteer work with the Fairfax County Commission on Transplants, an advocacy group that works with organ procurement organizations and hospitals. He gave talks in churches and to civic organizations about the need for donor organs in saving lives. He has counseled several people who are themselves candidates for organ transplants and are scared to death about it.

On January 18, 1997, my stepmother Deanne received a call from a young woman who asked if she had "the right number for the Jim Brehony who had a liver transplant at UVA in June of 1995." Bonnie Rangel, the donor's sister, was calling. Her family had received the letter from my father more than a year and a half earlier, and had just made photocopies of it. On the copies, my father's name and address could be faintly seen, although they had been whited out, and Steven's family now knew the identity of the recipient of his liver.

Five months later, my family met, for the first time, with Steven's family. We shared a meal and learned about Steven—his personality, his dreams, and what he had wanted from life. His mother Carol had brought pictures of him, and I was astounded to see his strong resemblance to my father's brother Bill, who died in 1953. The day was also a planned celebration at UVA Medical Center of thirty years of organ transplantation. It fell two years, almost to the day, after the death of a young man who is much in my heart but whom I will never know. I knew there were others, somewhere, holding similar celebrations. Carol's unselfish decision at her hour of wrenching grief had also given new life to two young people who were no longer shackled to dialysis and were thriving after kidney transplants, and someone else had been given a new pancreas, and yet another person had a new heart.

After the meal was over, we held hands in a circle, and my father, with tears running down his face, told Steven's family of all the wonderful things he had experienced in his life over the previous two years thanks to their compassion and generosity at such a heartbreaking time. He spoke about his grandson's high school graduation, the birth of Deanne's first grandchild, watching his granddaughter grow from a child into a lovely young woman, and the publication of his daughter's first book. All of these things, he told them, would have been lost to him without their gift. "I always wondered," Carol said, "if I had made the right decision. You never know really what you should do. But meeting you and your family has settled the question for me and given me peace." At that moment we felt as connected as any group of people could be. It was an amazing feeling that opened my heart and allowed everything that was not contained in that sacred and radiant moment to be suspended.[5]

Unlike other organs, kidneys may be donated by a living person. People are typically born with two kidneys but can live normal, healthy lives with one. It is not difficult to understand why someone would donate this critical organ to a family member or very close friend. It is harder to fathom why a person would make such a sacrifice for a stranger or casual acquaintance.

Like my father had been, Larry Wynn was dying. One of his kidneys had entirely ceased to function, and the other was barely working. He was on dialysis fifteen hours a week. This forty-eight-year-old financial analyst with General Motors was running out of time. His life depended on a kidney transplant, and, luckily, his sister had agreed to donate one of her kidneys. Larry was excited and hopeful about the chance to really live again. But within two weeks of his sister's decision, everything had changed. A series of tests had confirmed that she did not meet the criteria to be a donor for Larry. "I was very down," Larry told me. "I had my hopes up that something would work. My father had died only eight days before and I was so sad."

The same day that he learned that his sister couldn't be the donor, Larry's work took him to General Motors headquarters in Detroit. Larry normally works in Pontiac, about thirty miles away. When he got to headquarters, he stopped by to see his old friend Sal Petras, but Sal had gone to lunch. Larry and Sal had worked together at GM for more than eighteen years and were close as colleagues go, but not best friends. They played softball together on the company team and went with other co-workers to football and baseball games.

At around one, Larry was getting ready to drive back to Pontiac, but something compelled him to see if Sal was back from lunch. "I can't explain it, but for some reason I just couldn't leave the building," he says. "I saw a few other people, and then I went to take the elevator to leave, but I pushed the other button and went back upstairs. When I got to his office, he was there."

Sal immediately saw that Larry seemed very unhappy. Larry told him about his sister's not being able to donate her kidney. Sal pushed his chair back and told Larry that he wanted to try to donate one of his kidneys. "I said, 'Sal, this is serious. It's no joke.'" Sal said he was being completely serious and asked Larry for the telephone number for the transplant coordinator at Henry Ford Hospital. Larry still thought he was kidding and left to drive back to his office.

"I've known Larry since 1978," Sal told me. "He had chronic kidney disease that was made worse by hypertension. His kidneys were failing. When he found out that his sister couldn't donate, he was very down. To get that close and then be let down was devastating for him. I could see it in his face, heard it in his voice. I felt for him and put myself in the same position. We're about the same age. I couldn't imagine knowing that my life was going to end." Recalling the moment in his office, Sal said, "Something came over me. It is so unlike me to set my mind to do something like that. To this day I believe I was touched by God. But Larry is a friend and I knew I could help."

Sal went home that night and talked with his wife. He told her he wanted to donate a kidney to Larry. "She supported me a thousand percent," he says. "Larry is such a giving guy and had done so much to help minority youth through Big Brothers/Big Sisters and his church. It was hard to see him as sick as he was and not being able to do all the good things that he had done previously. We both felt that if there was something that I could do to help him I should do it."

The next morning, Sal called the transplant coordinator and made arrangements to begin the long process of testing required to determine if he could be a match for Larry. That afternoon, the coordinator called Larry to tell him that Sal was beginning the tests. "I started crying on the phone," Larry said. "It really came down on me about the kind of person he is over the eighteen years I've known him. I didn't think he was serious, and I didn't know if it would work because it's a cross-racial match. On my drive to work every morning I was overcome with joy and tears. I can't express my overwhelming joy that a friend—not a family member—would give that much to me."

Sal never wavered in his belief that his kidney would be a perfect match for Larry. "From the minute I decided what I wanted to do, I knew that everything was going to work out. Maybe it was blind faith, but I knew everything would be fine."

The tests confirmed that Sal could donate a kidney to Larry. Because Larry is black and Sal is white, the experts put the operation's chance of success at around eighty percent. Cross-racial transplants are rare—in 1997, only twenty-four such living kidney donations were performed nationally.[6] But even the lack of strong precedence for this kind of kidney donation did not diminish Sal's strong feeling that everything would work out well.

"My wife and I went on a vacation," Sal told me. "I did a little cross-training for my kidney down in the Keys." After he returned, they went ahead with the surgery on April 17, 1996. After the operations, Larry and Sal shared a hospital room. Sal was released after about four days and Larry was out in a week.

Today Larry is fully recovered and thriving. He told me that the transplant has never given him a moment of trouble and that the doctors had even reduced the amount of anti-rejection drugs that he takes. "I never even had any of that 'moon-faced' look, the side effects that people talk about having with steroids," he now says.

"It changed me spiritually," Sal says. "I am more cognizant of the presence of God. I seem to turn to Him more often when I need to sort things out, or have something on my mind. I was raised Roman Catholic and always had a close relationship with God, but mostly I went to church 'cause that's what you had to do. I get more out of it now and have private conversations with God. I have a more direct line," he says with a laugh.

Larry and Sal, once merely office buddies, have become the best of friends. "I never had a brother," Sal says. "Now I do. In fact, we're like one big family now and it's really nice. It's a good feeling."

They both say, and their wives agree, that they now have an almost "witchy" intuition about each other. Each says that he gets a strong feeling if the other one is having a bad day and will pick up the phone to see what's going on. In her book *A Change of Heart*, Claire Sylvia, a heart and lung transplant recipient, describes how the name of her organ donor came to her in a dream and she soon noticed that many of her attitudes, habits, and tastes had changed.

At one time a macrobiotic-eating, herbal-tea-sipping New Age modern dancer and teacher, she suddenly felt the urge to have a cold beer and some fried chicken.[7] One doesn't need to grasp all the dynamics of cellular memory or intelligence to understand how Larry and Sal developed a new closeness and intuition about each other.

Sal is quick to minimize the generosity of his gift to Larry. He is much more excited about the ripple effect that it seems to have created. He gets letters from friends and strangers telling him that this story has renewed their faith in mankind. "I've got friends who have told me that they had been thinking about donating bone marrow and that now they're definitely going to do it." Sal grew up in a large Italian family in New York that he describes as "warm and loving." There was nothing that family members wouldn't do to help each other. "Nobody ever sat down and preached that, they just did it. I always had as role models people who were generous and giving. In my case, I simply took it one step beyond family to someone who is a good friend."

"Larry is always saying he wants to repay me," says Sal, "but he doesn't have to. He can't. We look after each other now, and it feels like our families have blended. Besides, when you can help somebody else it's empowering. No one is holding a gun to your head—you do it willingly. And there is a sense of freedom and power that comes with that. It may sound kind of hokey, but it gives credibility to the idea that we're all brothers. There is an interdependency on each other, whether we recognize it or not.

When you look at the whole history of mankind, if you step back a little bit, you can get a good appreciation of it. What can be more important than having a positive impact on other people?"

Miki Hsu Leavey, of Napa, California, was stunned to find out that her kidneys were shutting down. Although she had been very sick with lupus from age nineteen until she was thirty-one, the disease had been in remission for almost twelve years, and during that time she had gotten used to being active and healthy. She didn't expect to find out anything remarkable when she went for her annual blood test. But the news was heartbreaking. Her kidney function had been worsening over the years, but it had happened in such small, consistent increments that doctors had failed to notice the trend until her blood counts were at a level that required immediate intervention. A sonogram confirmed her worst fears. She had four to five years before her kidneys would no longer function. Her doctors began to talk about dialysis and, ultimately, a kidney transplant.

"My sons were seven and nine at the time of this news. I assumed that there was a real possibility that I could die. It was a very frightening time. I didn't understand it because I was still feeling okay. I guess after so many years of being ill, I had developed a high pain tolerance, and unless I'm really sick I just don't want to slow down. The doctors thought that maybe my body just kept adjusting and compensating for the slow changes in my kidney function," she said.

The doctors' estimates were not correct; Miki didn't get a four-to-five-year reprieve. Less than a year and half later, she needed dialysis. "We did some radical things. I had always wanted to go to Europe, but I had been sick all through my twenties and then the children were born. My husband Lance and I thought it was something we would do when they were grown. But now that might not be a possibility. We couldn't afford it, but we charged everything and said, 'Let's go!' "

By the end of their trip to Europe, Miki was getting very sick. She was in end-state renal disease, and a kidney transplant was needed. Everybody in her large Chinese family stepped forward to donate: her mother, sister, five cousins, and an aunt. Her husband Lance was tested first. Despite their great love for her, no one in the family could donate. None even got past first base: a blood-type match is the first and most fundamental criterion for donating organs, and no one in Miki's family shared her type. Miki's blood type, O-positive, is the most common, but this actually worked against her. Since O-positive is the "universal donor" type, cadaver kidneys of this blood type can be given to people with blood types A, AB, and B; but Miki could *only* accept a kidney from an O-positive donor. The list of people waiting for kidneys is long in this country; more than 30,000 people are on it, and are either dying or on dialysis. Miki was placed on the national organ-recipient list, but doctors estimated at least a three-year wait for a kidney, and she wouldn't live that long without dialysis.

Miki was shattered when she learned that no one in her family could donate a kidney, but she didn't let it slow her down. She had two kids to care for. One day, on the way home from the hospital, she stopped by her bank. "I must have looked devastated," she remembers. Her bank teller, Mary Groves, asked her what was wrong, and Miki told her she had just gotten back from the UC San Francisco Hospital and then spilled out the rest of her story. Mary didn't even know that Miki had been sick; they would never have had occasion to discuss something like that. Miki says, "We were over-the-counter kind of friends. She worked at the same bank for years and we would chat about the weather and stuff like that. Mary is a dancer and I'm an artist so we did have some conversations about grants for the arts—Mary knew I had been able to win some grants, because of the kinds of checks I would deposit. But we didn't really know each other, had never even had a cup of coffee together."

Mary casually asked her how you went about donating a kidney. Miki told her, "Except for the fact that it has to match my blood type, I don't have a clue."

"What is your blood type?" Mary asked.

"As soon as she said her blood type and I knew that it matched mine, it felt almost like electricity going through me and I knew at that moment that I had to try," Mary said. "I felt led by God to try. That thought kept running through my head. And from that moment, I knew that it would work out—I had such a strong feeling about it. I didn't want to let on to Miki that I was even considering it, but in that split second I knew that I would." As soon as Mary got home from work, she called the hospital, tracked down the transplant team, and asked to be sent information and an application. She never mentioned anything to Miki; she didn't want her to get her hopes up, in case her own instincts were wrong and she couldn't donate.

Two weeks later, Miki went to the hospital for tests. She felt that her mother's intense anxiety might be calmed by talking with some people on the transplant team, so she brought her along. They arrived early and went to the transplant office to wait for the testing. The transplant coordinator said, "So, Miki, tell me about this Mary who wants to be your donor."

Miki was shocked. "Mary who?" she said. "I don't know any Mary."

The transplant coordinator looked through her file. "She's a friend. Mary. She's a bank teller, a dancer."

"Oh, my God," Miki said, and burst into tears.

After the tests, Miki went to the bank; she was told that Mary had the day off. As she turned to leave the bank, Mary came in the front door. She was there to do her own personal banking. When Miki saw her, she cried for the second time that day. "Oh, they told you," Mary said.

Three weeks later the two women were listening on phones at Miki's house, waiting to hear the results of the final test, which would determine if Mary could be Miki's donor. The doctor told them that they were a perfect match. Mary realized that this result proved that her original feeling was correct. "It confirmed for me that I was on the right track. I really felt that I was hearing from God. It was overwhelmingly exciting, but I wasn't surprised.

I wasn't even afraid of the surgery. I had complete faith that everything would be fine."

Four awkward months went by after that. Miki was afraid that Mary had changed her mind, but didn't want to push her if she were having second thoughts. In fact, Mary was simply putting things in order: moving to a new house, talking with her teenage son Ben about her decision, and telling Ben's grandparents about her plans. She was building the support systems that she would need during the recuperation period following surgery. Some of Mary's friends told her that they had some issues with her decision. "What if something happens to you during the surgery?" they asked her. "You're a single parent and Ben needs you. What if someday Ben needs a kidney?"

"I knew that both Miki and I were going to be fine," Mary says. "If Ben ever needed a kidney, I knew that God would make provisions for him just as He was doing for Miki. We can't live in a world filled with what-ifs. We would always be living in fear and never leave the house. I knew that what I was doing was a leap of faith, but from the first minute I had total peace."

As a dancer, Mary is very much in touch with her body and in excellent health. She spent time getting in shape for the experience of the surgery. "I innately felt that I had to prepare my body for this. I made a mental connection. I knew that they were going to take the right kidney even though they said they usually take the left one. I started talking to my right kidney—I named it Katherine—telling it that it should rest and let the other one do more of the work." She asked Miki to welcome this kidney into her body. She talked to the left one and told it that things would be fine but that it would have to work just a little harder. Mary admits that these conversations may seem a little crazy and that she had never talked to her body parts before, but she somehow felt that it was a necessary part of the process. Later, X rays revealed that the transplant team was indeed going to take her right kidney, a departure from usual procedure.

On December 10, 1996, both women entered the UC San Francisco Hospital for the surgery. Miki's husband Lance took care of Mary's son Ben, and they developed a very special relationship—"like a big brother," Miki says. Miki's extensive network of friends and family adopted Mary as their own, and welcomed her and Ben into their lives.

Both Miki and Mary understand that the friendship that has evolved between them is unique. "Our friendship is built on this one act," Miki says. "It's like marrying someone you don't really know. We're learning about each other as we go." Even if Mary had not matched and been able to donate a kidney, Miki says that the generosity of the offer would have changed her life. "Every time you look at the news, some kid has just been beaten up or somebody has died," Miki says. "The world may be ugly, but I know something about generosity and I'll never forget that."

Mary is a devout Christian and takes her faith very seriously. "I ask myself always, 'What would Jesus do in this situation?' I haven't always done that, but I'm ready for it now. For a long time I've been asking Him to teach me his character. We're his arms and legs. God is love. It didn't click with me that there was anything special about giving my kidney to Miki just because she wasn't family or a close friend. God moved me to do it for her—there's a reason for that."

Although Mary is very clear about her spiritual beliefs, Miki has a more eclectic faith that emerges from a number of sources. Raised Roman Catholic, and with a devoutly Buddhist grandfather, she often reflects on the teachings of the Tao and, like Mary, is confirmed in her belief in a higher power or some universal force.

One day shortly after the surgery, Miki's husband Lance came running into the house shouting. A hawk had become stuck on the roof after a fight with some crows, and Lance had grabbed it. It was struggling in his arms, and he was yelling for someone to call the wildlife rehabilitators. After Lance had taken the bird to someone who could take care of its wounds, a friend of Miki's who studies Native American mythology came to their house. She told them that the hawk is considered a powerful symbol of healing. Miki felt a chill go through her. Later that night she had a dream in which the hawk came back and she said to it, "I don't know what to do to give back. Why do I deserve this?" The hawk answered, "I brought Mary because no one else could do it for you. But you are also here to give back to Mary." The next morning, she and her husband set up a trust fund for Ben's education. The Leaveys understood that nothing could ever repay Mary's gift of grace but still felt that they had to do something for Mary and her son, as a way of saying thank you. Miki says, "It comes to you but it goes out from you someplace else. This is the way the world works for everybody."

Miki's thoughts about the circle of life—how we get and then we give back—reflect the spiraling way that grace moves in the world. In each of these stories, compassion required action. It required making an unselfish decision in heartbreaking circumstances, as Carol Sprinkel did so that "some good could come out of a tragic situation," or doing something because, as both Sal Petras and Mary Groves explained, one felt drawn to act by some higher force, based on a feeling of closeness even with a casual friend. Our rational minds might ask why someone would undergo radical surgery, and the extraction of an organ from his or her own body, for a casual friend. When you look deeper, you see that in the cycle of grace, determining who has been giving and who has been receiving is not so easy. This is the giving-and-receiving cycle called *tonglen* that the Buddhists speak of. Carol, Sal, and Mary all felt "blessed" to have been able to do what they did.

They are not alone in feeling this way. Amy Doggette, a graduate student at Washington University Medical School, interviewed more than two hundred kidney donors throughout the United States. All of them reported experiencing an increase in life satisfaction as a result of their donation. "I became a poet after the experience," said one donor, and another said, "It was like giving birth—I felt like I contributed something important."

On the Internet, I found a wonderful short essay by Steven Blakeman, a man who by his own admission "gets queasy at just the smell of a doctor's office." Steven had donated a kidney to his sister Denise, who had suffered with Bright's disease since she was fifteen and who later posted Steve's essay on the Internet to help people understand what it means to be a kidney donor. He wrote: "My sister has called me more in the last few weeks than in all the years since she moved to California. I know she's just trying to show her thankfulness for what I did for her. She keeps trying to say thank you and I keep telling her that it's not necessary. Sometimes I think that I'm the one who needs to say thank you for the opportunity that I had to be a part of this miracle. It's enough to know that because of my kidney, she has a new lease on life; an opportunity to enjoy her young marriage. The health to care for her young son and be a mother to him. Just to know that each day for her can now be greeted with excitement and enthusiasm. She will have the same opportunity as I to travel and enjoy life, not being tied to a machine. Having the health and strength to take a walk without fatigue, and the list goes on. Yes, I'm the one who needs to be thankful for this privilege. . . . Love has conquered fear and anxiety, and the results have been overwhelming."

While all of these donors and donor families seem special, having done things that we might not even consider, social science research has shown that there is only one way in which kidney donors differ from nondonors, and that is that donors have greater faith in the basic goodness of people.[8] These scientific studies confirm what the great religions and spiritual traditions of the world have always taught: seeing others as good—precious, worthy, God-created beings—who are intimately related to us makes us *want* to help them in whatever ways we can. This desire to help, to act, comes not out of pity or sentimentality, but because one experiences a felt connection with others as living beings. For these people, as for others who express ordinary grace, the basic belief that people are good resonates with what Rabbi Israel Baal Shem-Tov wrote at the beginning of the eighteenth century: "Evil cannot proceed from God."

And what of the people whose lives have been saved? Miki and Lance Leavey have embraced Mary and Ben as part of their large, loving family, and have set up a trust fund for Ben's education; Larry Wynn continues his good work with disadvantaged minority youth; and Jim Brehony works tirelessly to educate his community about the gift of organ donation while helping other people—who might otherwise die—get past their fears about taking the journey that he took. Their gifts have given life, have forged new, deeply felt relationships, and have given them a new definition of family. All of these people seem to understand the nature of ordinary grace and how it allows goodness to ripple from one person to another. In the words of Protestant minister and writer Frederick Buechner, "The life I touch for good or ill will touch another life, and that in turn another, until who knows where the trembling stops or in what far place my touch will be felt."[9]

Love Changes Everything

Every child comes with the message

that God is not yet discouraged of man.

—Rabindranath Tagore

During twenty-five years of marriage, Bill and Susan Belfiore had built a wonderful life together. They had grown up near each other on Long Island and had been friends since grade school, and it was no surprise to anyone when they got married. Now, as a successful couple in their early forties, they had found the good life in an exquisite home on a hill overlooking Princeton, New Jersey. Susan loved the creative challenges in her profession as a practitioner of Hellerwork, a holistic bodywork therapy. Bill was happy and thriving in his career as a corporate bond broker. They were both in excellent health, had lots of friends, and had plenty of money to do the things that they enjoyed. Although they'd been unable to have a child together—they had tried various fertility treatments without luck—they had accepted this disappointment years earlier, and life was rich and exciting for them both. They didn't expect everything to change dramatically one evening in the summer of 1990 when they sat down to relax in front of their TV.

They caught the end of a segment of *Primetime Live*—a story about the terrible plight of Romanian children who had been diagnosed with HIV. Warehoused in a home for abandoned children, they were suffering badly: The institution was barely able to meet their basic needs for food and shelter, there was no one to care for or interact with the children, and, as a result, many of them were not developing language skills or even learning to walk. The TV program included an interview with Brother Toby McCarroll, who had traveled to Romania and been overcome with sorrow by the devastation of these children. Brother Toby is part of a lay Catholic ministry—the Star-Crossed Community, in Annapolis, California—which helps children, especially those with HIV and AIDS. Brother Toby spoke about how all of the children were struggling to deal with their terrible circumstances, but the image of one little girl particularly haunted him. At two and a half years of age, she was unable to speak or walk and weighed less than eight pounds. Seeing her in this condition inspired Brother Toby to return to Romania to find some way to help all of the children. He and a group of other concerned people decided to take a radical step. They would move to Romania, divide the cavernous institution into small apartments, and create family units, each with four or five children and one adult caretaker—a surrogate mother or father. It was hoped that the children would bond with each other and their caretaker and that these relationships would improve their health and development. Brother Toby asked his volunteers to make a six-month commitment to live in Romania as caretakers. He had only three simple criteria: Volunteers had to be adaptable, able to put up with a difficult situation, and ready to cry a lot.

Susan and Bill were both powerfully moved by what they saw, and when the segment ended they discussed what they could do. It was a major commitment for both of them, but there was never a debate, never a moment of doubt. They both believed that they were in a unique position to do something for these children. They had the financial resources to allow Susan to take a leave of absence from her practice and for Bill to visit her during the six months that she would be gone. Susan picked up the phone and called NBC, the network that had aired the program. Since thousands of people had called, Susan was told to write a letter to the Star-Crossed Community explaining why she wanted to volunteer.

Susan was one of only five volunteers selected for the first group from among the thousands of people who had written letters. In January 1991, she packed her bags and flew to Romania. She moved into the "apartment" that had been created in the children's orphanage. She was assigned to five children—three girls and two boys—between the ages of two and four, and her bonding with them began immediately. She didn't expect to fall in love so quickly.

After two months, Bill flew over for an extended visit, and he, too, instantly felt deeply connected to the children. He and Susan began to talk about their love for these kids. They even considered adopting one of them. "I was given these five children to take care of and we did what we were supposed to do. We bonded. Both Bill and I fell in love with these children. I couldn't imagine leaving them at the end of six months," Susan says.

"We thought about our lives and what's important," Bill says. "Working on Wall Street and making a lot of money is not what it's about. Does it really make any difference what kind of car you drive? Once we fell in love with these children, it was out of our hands. It was not about logical decisions. Love changes everything."

They decided to adopt *all five* of the children.

Both Susan and Bill hold strong spiritual beliefs and feel that we are all being taken care of, that we are given what we need. "I have a very strong sense of being loved and cared for by someone. I always want to be open so that when my direction is presented to me, I'll be willing and able to go that way. We are directed and given guidance and I look for those signs along the way," Susan says.

It seemed like everything in their lives had been moving toward this point. They were living in a big house with a huge yard, surrounded by acres of trees—far more space than the two of them needed. They loved the house, but never could quite figure out why they had bought it. It is a beautiful and interesting house, the kind you might see in the pages of *Architectural Digest,* but when they first saw it they had been looking for something much smaller, a townhouse. Susan laughs as she remembers the realtor telling her she had a "fun" house to look at. "I couldn't even ask any questions when we walked through it because it didn't fit anything that was in my mind, not consciously anyway," she says. "I just looked around and was mute."

"It was like things were being set up for us," Bill adds. "We had this big house and no one to fill it. We had the money to go forward with this. Everything was already in place."

"When we first heard about these children, I thought all of them had been abandoned by their families, and while that is mostly true, it is not entirely true," Susan says. One of the children had returned to live with his family. Susan then went to the other four children's parents and told them what she and Bill wanted to do. All of them agreed to the adoption. Most did so because they simply did not want to deal with an HIV-positive child, but at least one family gave up their child out of love, knowing that there would be access to good medical care and a better chance for a healthy life in the United States.

Getting permission from the children's parents was the first and, in hindsight, the easiest step of the process. Getting permission from the Romanian government was another matter. The adoption was initially denied by the president of the Romanian court, who said that the court couldn't understand why the Belfiores wanted to do this. Then the minister of health told Susan that children with HIV and AIDS were like apples on trees that will simply wither, fall off, and die—in other words, that these were "throwaway" children. The Belfiores were told that they would be foolish to take on this responsibility. Bill says that, from the outset, there was pure distrust of their motives, but he suspects that a kind of power trip on the part of the Romanian officials played a part in their difficulties, too. "They said no simply because they could say no," he says. "It's not like these children were going to have a good life there." Bureaucrats accused Bill and Susan of wanting the children for experiments or for their body parts. But the Belfiores refused to give up. And they knew that they had to make all of the adoptions perfectly legal, so that the children could never be taken away from them.

"I asked everyone I ran into to speak on our behalf—even someone from the Vatican—but nothing helped," Susan says.

"I think that Susan just wore them down," Bill says, laughing. "They wanted to get rid of us. We weren't going away no matter what they said or how long it took."

"It was the only way it could have happened," Susan adds. "I was the mother for these children—the attachments of the heart were already there. We were already in love with each other."

Finally, after a year and a half, it appeared that the Romanian government would relent and the American Embassy could deliver the necessary paperwork. Everything had been so unclear up until the last minute that the Belfiores couldn't make any advance plans. They bought airline tickets the night before they left, and even then, they weren't certain that they would be allowed to leave the country. Bill's company showed its support by buying the $6,000 worth of one-way tickets. In the end, the paperwork did come through, and Bill, Susan, their four children, and a woman who would be their nanny boarded a plane for America.

Four years later, I'm visiting their home in Princeton, New Jersey. As I get out of my car in the driveway, the kids all come over to say hello. They are on their way to go ice skating on a local pond and are very excited about it. They introduce themselves and shake my hand, saying that they are glad to meet me and hope that I will have a nice time talking with their parents but wouldn't I rather go skating with them?

As I look at these beautiful kids, their terrible hardships and the challenges of living with HIV are not at all evident. They look like three ordinary sisters and a brother going skating for the afternoon, like any other group of eight- or nine-year-olds dressed for the outdoors in coats and mittens. The little boy is wearing a New Jersey Devils hockey jacket and decides to show me his muscles. He flexes his arm. "Feel these!" he says, laughing and gritting his teeth.

Bill opens the door with a wide smile. He is holding a baby. In spite of medical opinions that said it was impossible, Susan became pregnant with their now year-old son, Aidan. The original plan had been for five children, after all.

Bill and Susan tell me about their kids. Despite their common backgrounds, they are all very different and their individual personalities have blossomed in this loving environment.

Nine-year-old Ramona is what both Bill and Susan describe as a "real" girl. "She loves to play with Barbies, and I think she'll turn out to be one of those California Valley Girls," Bill says. Susan says that when Aidan was born, Ramona had a very hard time when he cried. "She was very sensitive to it and would put her hands over her ears. I explained that babies have to cry and then I realized what was going on with her. I sat down and talked with her. I said, 'When you spend time in a crib and there are not enough people to help you it can be very hard. You heard babies crying and you couldn't do anything to help, and maybe it was even you crying, Ramona.' "

Ionut is very intelligent. Bill says he can figure anything out. The previous summer, Bill was putting a new headlight on the car, using very tiny screws. Ionut told his dad to hold on while he ran inside to get a sheet to lay on the ground, in case Bill lost the screws on the rock driveway. "This will make them much easier to find when you drop them," he said. We laugh about Ionut's extroversion and ease with people. "He showed me his muscles outside," I tell them. They nod—he does this often with guests. Like most eight-year-old boys, he's fascinated by Power Rangers and other superheroes. "He's quite cerebral," Bill says, "but you can tell he's all boy because he hogs the remote control for the TV all the time."

Mihaela is a very sensitive nine-year-old. She loves horseback riding and anything else physical: sports, bicycling, and skating.

She never sits still. Like the other children, she has been thriving, but it appears that she may have to begin taking AZT and other medications for her HIV. Susan and Bill have been understandably concerned about this. Most of the research on medications for HIV has been conducted on adults, and it is unclear what kind of effects they will have on children.

At seven, Danna-rica looks more like a five-year-old, but Bill says she is "incredible, and bigger than life." What she may lack in size is more than made up for by her magnetic and dynamic personality. Bill calls her "Astro-Terrestrial" and asks her what planet she comes from. "When she walks into a room, she takes over," Susan adds. Bill tells me that he took her to a hockey game the night before I visited, and wherever she went, people lit up and naturally gravitated to her. During the game, Bill had looked up at the large TV monitor over the middle of the rink. The camera was aimed at the audience, and there, in giant close-up, was Danna-rica. "It figures!" he told her. It is only right that Danna-rica should command such attention, for she is the same little girl who weighed less than eight pounds at two and half years, and who so haunted Brother Toby—which is what brought Susan and the other volunteers to Romania in the first place.

The Belfiores' house is filled with warmth and love. I hear the excitement in Susan's and Bill's voices as they talk about what their children have brought to their lives. The outstanding architectural features and stylish furnishings of their home now share space with plastic toys. I hear Aidan in the kitchen, singing and gurgling like babies do. Falcor, their golden retriever, is lying in a patch of sunlight on the hardwood floor. Bill's mother lives in a building on the property, so the kids have a loving and very convenient grandmother. All of this bustle is a far cry from Bill's and Susan's earlier life, and I ask just how much their lifestyle has changed since they became a family.

"What lifestyle?" Bill asks. "I don't *have* a lifestyle. I think I left my lifestyle in Romania. I sure hope someone found it and picked it up." We laugh together, and I realize how much we have all laughed during the course of this afternoon.

Like most people who display ordinary grace, Susan and Bill believe they are the ones that have been blessed. They are adamant in their feeling that they haven't done anything special. In fact, they suggest that I should really be talking with friends and acquaintances who have rallied round them to help the children adjust, and lent a hand when needed. These people are the ones, they say, who really express this ordinary grace that I'm talking about.

"We wanted a family and now we have one," Susan says, smiling. "These kids filled our needs. They needed a place to live and a better life than they had. We needed those children to share our lives with. It worked out. They are incredible, and our life right now is beyond anything we could have imagined. They bring aliveness into our lives and we never would have lived so fully without them. You know, love takes you places where your head would never go."

I have been blessed by being able to take part in a yearly retreat for people living with HIV and AIDS. This weekend event, called Transformation Retreat, offers a powerful experience for the people who attend. In the process of learning about themselves, they find an unexpected treasure; they begin as strangers and leave as a community of friends. Funded by contributions from individuals, churches, and synagogues, the retreat is organized and run by forty-one volunteers who work throughout the year planning and managing the program. Though non-denominational, it is held at the Roman Catholic Holy Family Retreat Center in Hampton, Virginia, a simple building with dorm-like rooms, a large kitchen, a dining area, and a meeting room looking out over a broad lawn that spreads down to Chesapeake Bay. Colorful panels are hung on the walls, made by participants from previous years. Many of these people have since died, and small, white paper butterflies have been attached to the panels they made, each attesting to the life and the passing of the person who made it.

The site is beautiful, with a wonderful view of the water, trees, and wildflowers. A patio with comfortable chairs is a perfect place to sit and talk, but hardly anyone goes there on the first night. Living with a life-threatening illness has taken its toll, and, never having been exposed to a retreat experience, most people arrive scared to death.

Tricia Hulsey, a close friend of mine, was involved in the creation of this retreat in 1990. "I felt compelled to address the needs of the AIDS epidemic because of my strong belief in social justice. We don't think about that much in this country—but there are so many people who live on the periphery of society. I spoke with my pastor at the Church of the Resurrection, and he said to pray about it and find my own direction." Tricia and four other people started Transformation Retreat "on a wing and a prayer," and that first year they opened the doors to twenty-eight people. The retreat organizers have watched as the demographics of the AIDS epidemic have shifted over time. "The first year it was almost all gay white men," she tells me. "Now, at least 50 percent of our retreatants are African-American and about one-third are women."

The forty-one volunteers work all year to plan four retreats that are held at various times throughout the state. They receive no salaries, have no offices, and incur no operating expenses except for the cost of printing brochures (which they design) and mailing them to churches, mosques, synagogues, AIDS clinics, and other organizations throughout Virginia. "Everyone who comes to the retreat is on scholarship. We arrange transportation when it is needed. We like to have flowers around during the retreats, and those are donated by local florists. Our special dinner is prepared by volunteers. We get speakers and workshop leaders who represent a broad spectrum of spiritual ideas—Jewish, Islamic, Buddhist, Native American, Christian. But we don't pay speakers' fees, and there are no honorariums. It's always an act of love from everyone. Each person who attends the retreat gets a little 'goodie bag' with shampoo, toothpaste, lotions and such. We usually get those from hotels, but last year the touring company from *Les Mis'* gave us piles of things—they had been on the road a long time and collected a lot of loot from the hotels they stayed in!"

The mission statement for Transformation Retreat sums up the purpose of the weekend: "Alone and together we seek to enter into the circle of life and energy which holds all things together." Tricia tells a moving story about the Friday-night talent show that is held at each retreat to loosen everybody up. This show is both humorous and touching, and includes everything from poetry readings and skits to a performance by someone who once danced with the Joffrey Ballet. One year, a young man named Mel dressed in drag and lip-synched to the song "From a Distance," as sung by Bette Midler. The lyrics speak of a time when there will be "no guns, no bombs, and no disease." Sitting in the back of the room was seventy-three-year-old Father Jerry, the priest who managed this very conservative Catholic retreat house. The crowd was moved enough by the song to hold hands in a circle and sing along. At the words "no disease," Mel threw his bottles of AZT medicine onto the floor. Everybody began to cheer, holding each other and crying. Father Jerry came from the back of the crowd and joined hands with the others. He knew when spirit was present. This traditional Catholic priest, from a much older generation, could sense the love and connection that existed there, even during a drag show. The next morning, he left a note on the message table for all to read. It said simply, "The grounds of this retreat house have never been so holy."

"Our retreat is spiritual but nondenominational," says Tricia. "We stress that everyone is coming here from diverse backgrounds. We want to stand together in the presence of spirit—

to be empowered in living. Everyone is transformed, including the people who organize it."

The participants in Transformation Retreat have discovered, through their common pain, how to really open their hearts to each other. No longer isolated, they have transcended the idea that each bears a separate sorrow. Within the compassionate forum of this weekend experience, not a barrier was left between them. Under "normal" circumstances, these people would have been unlikely to meet. They range in age from twenty to sixty, and represent all ethnic groups, races, sexual orientations, and economic and social spheres. Where else but in a place where love abounds could you find a middle-aged, professional, gay white man becoming best friends with a twenty-three-year-old straight African-American woman who is recovering from cocaine addiction and living in a public housing project? These improbable friends gather in *sangha*—a Buddhist word for "spiritual community"—and in so doing discover that a savage beauty surrounds them and gives them a renewed sense of dignity, and melts away all the differences between them.

The ordinary grace illuminated by the Belfiore family, and by the participants in the Transformation Retreat, speaks beautifully about the deep love and connection that can be found in the most unlikely places among people who don't appear to have anything in common. How is it that a highly successful couple from Princeton, New Jersey, can become parents to four abandoned Romanian children? How is it that people from all walks of life—and all engaged in a struggle with a terrible disease—can find friendship, community, and common ground at a weekend retreat?

Each of these stories is an affirmation of the ancient notions of the circle of life, of inclusion, and of welcoming. Every day, all kinds of people—children and adults with HIV/AIDS, the homeless, the disabled—are abandoned all over the world. Sometimes this exclusion takes a recognizably bureaucratic form: Imagine a Romanian official describing beautiful and remarkable children as apples that would fall from a tree, that would inevitably wither and die. Sometimes the exclusion is more subtle: We walk past someone who needs our help. We "don't have time" to go by and see our aging relative in a nursing home. We don't make an effort to become friendly with a new neighbor because she is the "wrong" color, or religion, or sexual orientation, or class. But grace refuses to accept these limits; when we live in grace, it becomes clear that *every* life is precious and deserving of our protection, our love, and our relationship.

When we open our hearts to each other we allow grace to enter. It is as simple as that. And suffering—events that break open the heart—can become the refiner's fire that leaves us fully open to the truth about love and compassion.

Rumi, a mystical Sufi poet writing in the thirteenth century, understood the riches that underlie suffering for those willing to open their hearts and look:

The most secure place to hide a treasure of gold
is in some desolate, unnoticed place.
Why would anyone hide treasure in plain sight?
And so it is said,
"Joy is hidden beneath sorrow."[1]

6.

Keeping the
Dream Alive

A human being becomes human through other human beings.

—Zulu proverb

An old man is dying and calls his family and neighbors together. He reaches into a large bag and hands each one of them a short, sturdy stick. Then he directs them to break the sticks. The sticks, though strong, are easily broken. Even the smallest child snaps hers in two.

"When a soul is alone without anyone else, it can be broken," he tells them.

The old man then hands everyone a new stick. "This is how I want you to live after I die," he says. "Put your sticks together in bundles of two or three or more. Now, break those bundles in half."

No matter how they try, no one can break the bundles. The old man smiles. "We are strong when we stand with another soul," he says. "When we are with another, we cannot be broken."

A Jungian analyst and writer named Clarissa Pinkola Estés was told this story by an old black man living in the mid-South. The story is called "One Stick, Two Stick," and it is the way, he whispered to her, of the old African kings.[1]

"We have got to stand together," says Gerri Hollins of Hampton, Virginia. "Nobody wins if we cannot help these children." Gerri, a middle-aged African-American woman with long dreadlocks and a dramatic voice, is talking to me at her home and studio in Hampton, Virginia. "There's a war going on with black kids," Gerri says. "I lived in New York, and the drugs were coming in like you wouldn't believe. Gangs control everything. Every few blocks are split up by different groups of people controlling the drug trade. Children, ten and twelve years old, carry guns. How can we teach them? How can we tell them to work hard and get a job, be a good person, when the drug gangs will pay them seventy-five dollars a day just for whistling when they see a police car?"

In the late 1970s, Gerri moved to New York to become a teacher at the Harlem School for the Performing Arts and to sing in the chorus at the Met. Within just a few years she became a singer and vocal coach for Sony/RCA Records. Her work put her in contact with performers from all over the world. But despite her success, she was still living in a neighborhood that was suffering. One day, a boy Gerri knew well came running over to her, calling out her name. "He came over and fell on me," Gerri says. "I said, 'What are you doing?' A great big old boy falling on me. He moved away and my dress was covered with blood. He had been stabbed twenty-six times. He died two hours later in Harlem Hospital." In 1985, in a single month, Gerri tells me, there were sixteen young men killed within a two-block radius. "They are out there in this concrete maze seeing the same drug dealers every day. I knew that there had to be some way to turn their minds around."

Shortly after the death of her young friend, three young boys asked Gerri for some money so that they could go to a theme park in upstate New York. She refused to give them money but told them she would help them earn some on their own. She invited them to her house and taught them how to bake cookies. "I come from a long line of chefs and cooks," she told the boys. Her grandfather had owned a bakery in Balti-more and her father was a professional chef. She taught the boys how to make cookies, pies, and cakes, and they sold their wares on the streets outside of City College. They earned $128 on their first day. They were so excited about their new skill and their ability to earn money from it that they began to tell their friends. Soon there were fourteen boys who wanted to learn about making cookies. The group had quickly outgrown Gerri's tiny kitchen.

She went to her church officials to ask if they would sponsor these kids and let them use the church's basement kitchen, which had been unused for more than seven years. She was asked to write a proposal and present it to the Deacon and the Deaconess Board. Their final word was: "We don't have any space for this."

"The community had become fearful of its own youth," Gerri says, shaking her heard as if she still cannot believe it. "I went to the church and the church turned me down so I went and talked to a friend." Gerri took her idea to the man who owned and managed the Cotton Club, and he told her, "Sure, no problem." She took the boys over to the club's kitchen, which also had not been used in years, and showed them the opportunity they now had. "I wanted to hear it from their mouths about what we could do with this kitchen. It was a wreck and needed one of those real 'grandma cleanings.' " But the boys were undaunted by the work in front of them. They scrubbed the walls, washed the floors on their hands and knees, and scoured every pot and pan. "We found a dead mouse behind the ice machine," Gerri remembers, "but we gave it a proper burial and then went on with the work."

The irony of being turned down by a church and embraced by a nightclub is not lost on Gerri. She was appalled at the church's shortsightedness, although she continues to hold strong religious beliefs. As part of the agreement to have Gerri teach them how to cook, all of the boys had to make a vow that they would stay away from drugs and violence and watch out for each other. They called themselves the "Little Brothers," and started baking and selling their cookies. Gerri supported them with money from her overseas concerts. She is one of the premier singers in Japan and Europe, places she still travels to several times a year, and sings everything from Baroque opera and oratorio to jazz and blues. People told her that she couldn't afford to take so much time away from performing to work with these kids, but she didn't listen. "You have to step out on faith," she says. "These kids are our primary source for the future, and we can't afford to let them slip away from us."

In 1991, Gerri returned to Hampton, to strengthen her commitment to black children in the neighborhood where she grew up. She formed the Hampton Apple Tree Club House, or HATCH, a program dedicated to providing a safe place for children to learn about themselves and each other. The program is enthusiastically intergenerational and multicultural, in the belief that young people must gain knowledge, understanding, and respect for other cultures.

Gerri took me to see the three Victorian houses that make up the HATCH program. She lives in one, and works there as a piano teacher and voice coach. Another house holds the Apple Tree Pantry Cookie Shop and Café, where the kids learn to bake cookies and the neighbors can come in and relax over a cup of cappuccino. Money generated from the café supports a Learning Center upstairs. Several rooms have been converted into classrooms with computers and printers. "This is the Computer Club," she says. "Most kids in this neighborhood don't have computers at home, so this is a place where they can learn about them, and come in and write their papers for school."

Another room is set up with desks and a chalkboard. Volunteers conduct a variety of classes for the kids: electronics, mechanical drawing, landscaping, marketing, business, and languages, including Japanese, Spanish, Swahili, Arabic, and Italian. Gerri's own love of the arts is connected to her strong belief that "creativity is our lifeline to the Creator." She believes that getting kids involved in creating art and expressing themselves is a powerful path to self-esteem and healthy values.

The third house has an international gift shop that supports the art studios upstairs, where kids make jewelry, design and sew clothes, paint, and sculpt. "You get these children involved in shows and making art and you help them keep their minds on loftier thoughts," Gerri says. She writes and produces several musicals each year. All of the shows have large ensemble casts, and this gives lots of kids the opportunity to perform. Two favorites have been "Wings over Harlem, Honey, and I Don't Mean Chicken" and "Mother Goose Cuts Loose." There were three young girls waiting to audition when I met with Gerri, each accompanied by her parents. Gerri requires parental participation in all of her productions. "The parents don't have to get on stage and sing if they don't want to, but they have to be part of it. They can make costumes, be stage managers, or build scenery, but I want them there with their children."

Gerri sees HATCH as an entrepreneurial training program that fosters quality education and cultural enrichment and promotes positive imagery and strong relations between youth and adults from different backgrounds. HATCH promotes a yearly retreat in which young people from all over the world come together to study and interact. "I want to dispel the myths about African-Americans," she says. "Some people have failed to see that our kids are not just doing drugs and crime. Last year a group of young Japanese people came to one of our retreats. They wanted to get to know how we lived, how we eat, how we go to church. I took them to see how the slaves lived and then the ways in which black people have contributed to American society. One boy in the group could only speak a little English when he came here. But he graduated cum laude from his school and was accepted at four graduate schools in the United States. He wrote me to tell me that he was going to study African-American history and culture. He will be one who can tell the truth about what's going on when he returns to Japan after his schooling."

Gerri recounted growing up on the same streets of Hampton where the kids in HATCH live. "When I was a kid, Grant Street was a village. Kids respected older people. They might be walking down the street cursing their heads off but when they were in front of my grandmother's house it was 'How you doin', Miss Leanna? Pretty day, isn't it?' My grandmother never called anyone a bum. There was no one who couldn't get a meal if he needed it. She'd say, 'Go out and pick up that man.' And we'd pick him up. He may have been down on his luck but he was still part of our world. He wasn't a bum, he was Good Gin, Hot

Pappa, Big Apple, Sneaky Pete, String of Pearls, Brown Sugar, Four Corners, or Head Light. My grandmother knew them all. She'd tell them to get cleaned up and then give them something to eat. Then she'd sit them down and read them the Word."

Gerri remembers the time when people in the neighborhood knew and cared about each other in the same ways her grandmother did for those guys down on their luck. "When I was growing up, there was a feeling of community, of belonging. If you did something wrong, before you got home, your mama knew about it. That's the village. That's community. We needed it then and these kids need it now."

John Horton has never met Gerri Hollins, but they are reading from the same page. Born in Chattanooga, Tennessee, fifty-seven years ago, John quickly learned what it's like to be poor and have no future to look forward to. As the oldest of five black children, born to a mother who dropped out of school in the second grade and a father who abandoned the family, John grew up in a housing project, and it seemed to him as if he would live and die in a project just like it. His mother worked eleven-hour days as a housekeeper earning seventy-five cents an hour. Despite her poverty and lack of schooling, John's mother always taught her children the importance of an education. "By the second grade," he says, "I had learned to read because my mother read to me from the comic pages every day. She was not an educated woman, but she taught me to read. I remember Dick Tracy, Little Orphan Annie, Little Lulu, Gasoline Alley, Smilin' Jack Burnett, and Rex Morgan. I was fascinated by those cartoon characters and wanted to read the captions."

In grade school, John was an honor student, but he was still ashamed of his poverty. He wore shoes that had cardboard for soles, and some days he had no lunch at all. The other children made fun of him—most of them were also poor, but not as poor as he was. "When I got to be about fourteen, in the ninth grade, I was still on the honor roll but I was feeling more and more like I didn't belong there," he told me. "I guess the hormones kicked in. I wanted the girls to like me. The other boys had nice tennis shoes and nice trousers. I had the same old pair of blue jeans that I washed and ironed every day. But at that age, I didn't understand things very well, and the teasing got to be a little too much."

At sixteen, John admits, he was going nowhere. He had dropped out of school and taken odd jobs—cutting grass, shoveling coal, and picking cotton and fruit to make a little money. At seventeen, he went to a Marine Corps recruiting office and took the test to enlist. "I still believe that this was the turning point in my life," he says. "It was a blessing. If I hadn't gotten out of the projects I would be dead, in jail, or homeless by now. I feel like my background made me tough, able to appreciate the hard times and know that I wanted something better in my life."

While most of the young Marine recruits complained about the difficulties of boot camp and the discipline it required, John thought he had died and gone to heaven. "I got shoes, a uniform, and a regular paycheck. I made thirty-three dollars every two weeks and could afford to send money home." For the first time in his life, he found a place where everyone was treated equally. The sergeants yelled at everyone—black men, white men, and brown men. John was in excellent physical shape, was smart, could read well, and was beginning to understand that the Marine Corps might be his only hope of finding a way to a better life.

During his early years in the Marines, his intelligence and motivation were recognized by a captain in his company, who requested that John become his aide, an unheard of opportunity for a "colored" Marine in the 1950s. John's talents were also later noted by a sergeant from Boston who simply would not tolerate racism in his ranks. Although both of these men were white, they became mentors to John in an era of great racial conflict and segregation, even in the military. "I always think about him," John says about his captain, "and realize that he didn't have to do that. He gave me opportunities and helped me to see that I could be somebody. The most important people in my life have been those who treat people right even when they don't have to. These two guys gave me reason to believe in myself. They knew that I had potential."

John completed thirty years of active service in the Marines, and by the time he left had been promoted to sergeant major— the highest enlisted rank. During the course of his military career, he earned his high school GED, an associate's degree, two bachelor's degrees, and a master's degree in human relations. John is now retired from the military and works with disadvantaged youth through the Restorative Justice Program for the juvenile court system in Norfolk, Virginia. He teaches these kids, almost all of whom live in what he calls "the island of public housing," the importance of remaining in school, staying away from drugs, avoiding unwanted pregnancies, and keeping their lives clean and filled with promise. He was recently honored with the Federal Law Enforcement Officers Association's highest award, and named Civilian of the Year for his work with at-risk kids in the community.

"I don't believe in victims," he says. "I don't believe in being nobody and I don't believe in being useless. I do believe that whatever is to be is up to the individual, regardless of his or her circumstances. You've got to make the best of your life—it's the only hand of cards you're going to be dealt, so you get out there and do the best you can."

John is a firm taskmaster with his kids—thirty years in the Marine Corps has taught him the value of discipline and responsibility. One program he developed targets sixth- through eighth-graders from disadvantaged families in two of the public housing projects in his city. For kids in this community, truancy and absenteeism increase dramatically between elementary and middle school, and the goals of the program are to have the students attend school ninety percent of the time, to get them to maintain at least a 2.0 grade point average, and to encourage parental participation in their children's attendance. "The overwhelming reason I found for students not going to school was that there was no one strong enough, tough enough, with enough conviction to make that child get up and go to school," he says.

"Most of these kids have no relationship at all with their fathers. Here is the statistic: In 1910, 90 percent of all black households were headed by a man and a woman who were legally married. In 1960, it was 80 percent, and in 1990 it's less than 40 percent. Any ethnic group that loses half of the family, and the partnership that the man provides to his wife in raising children, is in deep trouble. Most of these kids have never heard a deep masculine voice saying, 'Boy, you don't talk to adults like that.' Mothers have had to play both parental roles."

Although John grew up without a father, he remembers what he was taught by uncles, grandfathers, and other men in his community. Recognizing that kids today generally don't have those kinds of role models, John is developing mentoring programs for young men and women where they can learn self-esteem, self-respect, and personal empowerment. Left on their own, these kids find their own ways of coping. For girls, that often means getting pregnant. For boys, it usually means an unrestrained masculinity that may be expressed in violence, joining a gang, or getting a girl pregnant. "A man is judged by three things," he tells his boys, "how he treats women, how he treats young ones, and how he treats his elders. And that goes for all men—black, white, brown, or any other color."

John may be tough, but he loves these kids and understands the odds they are working to overcome. "If a society conditions people to be dependent, to be subordinate, to believe that they can't achieve anything, then they will surely live up to those ideas. If I fall in a hole all by myself, that is my fault. But if you dug the hole and pushed me toward it, well maybe it wasn't all my fault. Society has a responsibility to close up all the holes that are left, and then we can play ball on a level playing field. After that, it's up to the individual to make something of his or her life."

John has no bitterness about growing up black in the 1940s and 1950s. He feels that most of the young people he works with today fail to appreciate how far African-Americans have come over the last thirty years. "These kids were always allowed to go to McDonald's, sit in the front of the bus, work for the city, join the military, or go to college."

He has no desire to revisit the old days, but like Gerri Hollins, he regrets the loss of community that once existed even in very poor black neighborhoods. "Once upon a time," he says, "we had more dignity, more strength, more togetherness than we have now in spite of all the name changes we've experienced. My birth certificate says colored on it. Now we call ourselves black or African-American. But there was power and substance in those communities. Some of the poorest people I've ever met were the salt of the earth. Dignity, honesty, determination, stamina, never saying quit, and working hard are the things that I learned—those values have nothing to do with class, education, or income—and they were prevalent in most poor communities, black and white. People hung together, and I wouldn't be where I am today without their shoulders to stand on. Many of the kids today seem to have lost that sense of toughness, strength, and love."

For all of the problems of America's youth, especially those living in poverty, we often neglect to focus on what is going right for these kids. The love and grace that are pouring into communities are changing things.

In Suffolk, Virginia, fifth-graders are tutoring kindergarteners after school in reading, writing, and math. In Norfolk, junior varsity and varsity basketball players are tutoring elementary school students. Interestingly, but not unexpectedly, everyone's grades have gone up—both those being tutored and those doing the tutoring. In Washington State, Hannah Hawkins tends to neglected children after school with tough mothering, lessons, and meals. "If you get them at a young age, you can help mold them," she says. In Greensboro, North Carolina, volunteers work with teenage mothers to help them develop parenting skills. In Chicago, women have donated business suits and dresses, many of them expensive designer fashions, to the Bottomless Closet. Young women attempting to get off welfare can go there to get clothes appropriate for job-hunting and the workplace. In 1989, African-American fathers in Omaha, sick of losing their sons and daughters to gangs and gang violence, formed a group called Mad Dads to patrol street corners, serve as surrogate fathers, and host positive events for local kids. The original group of eighteen Omaha men has grown to more than 25,000 members, with forty-one chapters in the poverty zones of eleven states.

Helen Ramey started tutoring inner-city kids in Los Angeles in 1969 in her church basement. Now, at seventy-eight, she has moved into another building to accommodate the many volunteers who work one-on-one with more than six hundred kids each year.

In Houston, Carol Porter makes hundreds of sandwiches every day in her small kitchen, so that poor kids will have a good lunch. She understands that it's hard to learn if you're hungry and your stomach is rumbling. In New York City, eighty-one-year-old Marie Runyon has been called a "rabble-rouser" for taking miserable apartment buildings out of the hands of dishonest landlords through her Harlem Restoration Project. Rodney Dailey scours the streets of Boston's poorest and most violent neighborhoods for kids in danger of joining gangs. A former gang member and drug abuser himself, he got clean, finished college, and then founded Gang Peace in 1989. Since then, Rodney and his volunteers have reached out to more than 20,000 kids through workshops, mediation, and mentoring. In Kansas City, Missouri, G. G. Owens and other "block leaders" offer latchkey kids a place to go after school. Serving as surrogate mothers and fathers, these volunteers provide a place where kids can have cookies and milk and someone will inquire about their day at school. Block leaders take these children on field trips to museums, teach classes in art and crafts, and get them involved in community service. "We're making a difference," G.G. told me. "We're providing all kinds of interesting and fun things for kids to do. Giving them a caring adult to learn from. They aren't hanging out on the street corners now—the word is out, this is the place to be."

Many of these young people, having been helped, recognize the need to put something back into their own communities. Record numbers of high school and college students are now performing volunteer community service. A national survey conducted by Independent Sector, a nonprofit coalition of corporate foundations and voluntary organizations, reported that black teens are volunteering more than any other segment of the population.[2]

Melvin Elliott, an eighth-grader from Norfolk, Virginia, has spent his whole summer, six hours a day, six days a week, volunteering to help elderly residents at the Sentara Nursing Center. He plays games with the residents, brings their lunch on trays, and wheels them outside to the garden, where he will spend hours sitting and talking to them. "I like their smiles," he says, "and they can tell you about stuff that happened a long time ago." Melvin is the oldest of six children being raised by an aunt and uncle because his parents are unable to take care of him. But he's a straight-A student and is tutoring some of the children of the Sentara staff. He plans to come to the nursing center after school and on weekends once his classes begin again in the fall.[3]

April Reyes, a high school student in Norfolk, didn't think it was fair that pizza restaurants wouldn't deliver to the Roberts Village public housing project. "It's too violent," the companies said. "We don't deliver to high-crime areas." April and four of her friends decided to start a company that would make deliveries to residents, many of whom are elderly and have no means to go out and get a meal. "They're just high school kids, and they wanted to bring back a simple pleasure to the community," said Jackie Baker, youth services coordinator for the Norfolk Redevelopment and Housing Authority. Calling themselves Pizza-Ria! and using the motto "It's fresh! It's good! It's from the 'hood!" these teenagers have earned more than $15,000, helped send one teenager to college, and brought a sense of pride and respect to their neighborhood.[4]

Most people living in the midst of poverty, violence, drugs, and hopelessness feel overwhelmed. If ever there has ever been a need for a community-wide effort to find solutions and act on them, this is where it must start. But even here, in the dark alleys of the inner city and the dusty roads leading to pockets of rural poverty, ordinary grace is present. Take the stories of Gerri Hollis and John Horton: Here are talented, educated, motivated people who could do many different things with their lives. Each one has chosen to give something back—to work to bring back the sense of community and belonging that they remember from their own lives. But Gerri and John are not alone. My files and notebooks overflow with stories of ordinary grace that come from some of our most desperate communities. It is clear that a new consciousness is rising up, a harkening back to the old days where neighbors took care of neighbors. People are discovering that they can pull together and begin to solve the problems that confront them. Ordinary grace loves the vernacular, the earthy, the present, the real. It is not necessary to travel the world to find or express ordinary grace. In fact, it is most important to start where we are: right here, right now, in our own communities. These stories make clear how people—of all ages, races, and faiths—are learning to work together, to stand together. Like the bundles of sticks from the old man's bag, together they cannot be broken.

7.

Healing Broken Places

Do not be overcome by evil, but overcome evil with good.

—Romans 12:21

A plane lands and the doctors and medical staff aboard gather their carry-on luggage and head for the door. These physicians, medical technicians, and nurses have come from throughout the United States, Canada, Europe, and elsewhere, but this is no ordinary junket, no medical convention at a tony resort; these doctors won't be spending any time on the golf course. Instead, these men and women, who specialize in plastic surgery, cardiology, oral surgery, dentistry, nursing, anesthesiology, and general surgery, are donating their time and talent to provide medical care and training thousands of miles from their homes. As volunteers with Physicians for Peace, they will be spending the next two weeks in grueling hours of surgery and patient care, teaching new medical procedures to foreign colleagues and students, and falling exhausted into bed at a modest hotel or, perhaps, in a sleeping bag at a campground. By the end of the first day some of them will have treated more than ninety patients on Israel's war-torn West Bank.

Founded in 1984 by plastic and reconstructive surgeon Charles Horton, Physicians for Peace, or PFP, promotes international friendship and peace through medicine.[1] Although these volunteer missions have focused a great deal of energy on the turbulent Middle East, they have also been dispatched to South and Central America, the Far East, Africa, the Caribbean, and Eastern Europe. The organization is definitely apolitical, secular, and nonprofit, dedicated only to improving health care throughout the world and making friends in the process. Based on a philosophy of mutual respect, PFP emphasizes the importance of sharing medical knowledge so that local doctors can continue to provide advanced medical care to their patients on their own, long after the volunteers have returned home. "We like the ripple effect," Charles Horton tells me. "It's like the Chinese proverb that says if you give a man a fish you feed him once, but teach a man to fish, he will feed himself for the rest of his life."

Illness and the desire for healing are great equalizers in our human community and form a common ground upon which we can build enduring relationships and learn to work together to solve the tremendous health problems around the world. "Regardless of race, religion or geographic location," Charles says, "the tears of a mother, the cries of a young child, and the disabilities of a father are the same."

Charles also knows that although people are the same all over the world, it takes personal contact to break down the stereotypes and form bonds that can transcend the politics of international relations. He told me about a conversation he once had with a man who had very negative feelings about Muslims. "I told this man, 'Do you know that almost one hundred percent of Muslims are more religious than we are? They're kind, they love their children, they want them to be educated and to sleep in peace. They pray for peace just like we do; you know that the great majority of Americans are not the militia, bombers, or people who start riots. Yet that's the kind of news that people throughout the world hear about us. We have to counteract that view with respect and friendship—by forming relationships with good people throughout the world.' "

The idea of using the human need for medical care as a bridge for creating understanding and brotherhood—of making doctors into civilian diplomats—came to Charles more than twenty years ago. Through his affiliation with Eastern Virginia Medical School in Norfolk, he had worked with many doctors from other countries and had witnessed friendship's power to break down barriers. Amazingly, some of the most powerful relationships he watched develop were between people who, in their home countries, would be considered mortal enemies, some of them divided by declarations of war. "I saw so many examples of people holding their 'enemy's' child on their lap and telling them

'I hope that you never have to fight like we had to fight.' People are the same all over the world: When they get to know each other, they respect and enjoy each other. It works."

Charles had no trouble finding doctors who would commit to helping people abroad; most of the physicians he knew would readily volunteer to teach foreign colleagues and offer their medical expertise to suffering people in other countries. But he realized, too, that some kind of structure would be necessary for deploying these people. It would be impossible for any individual doctor to stand on a street corner in Damascus and offer his or her services. "The people there wouldn't know them or their credentials. They wouldn't know if they were capable or crazy," Charles says. In spite of good intentions, a surplus of interested volunteers, and the tremendous demand throughout the world for quality medical care, doctors and nurses needed an organization that could manage these missions of teaching and compassion.

Since 1984, PFP has sent more than one hundred fifty medical teams to dozens of countries, but it has reached only a small fraction of the billions of people throughout the world who desperately need the help of modern medical skills and technology. In fact, the health-care needs of the world are so vast that even if every American doctor donated all of his or her professional time, it would be only a "drop in the bucket," Charles says. A surgeon may perform a hundred operations on children with birth defects in a single medical mission, but, he says, it is common to find that during the same mission the number of deformed babies born in that country is greater than the number of those who were helped.

PFP believes that the best way to tackle this problem is to teach other doctors to take care of their own, and therefore the group places a high premium on the education of foreign medical professionals. They do this through observational teaching, by organizing symposia on cutting-edge medical techniques, and by bringing some of the doctors and nurses to the United States, as "visiting scholars," for further study and practice. In every case, the emphasis is on establishing interaction and shared responsibility between PFP medical professionals and their colleagues from other nations.

One place where PFP has had a lasting impact is Nicaragua. Cervical cancer has long been one of the leading causes of death among women there. Yet although the disease is easily cured if it's caught at an early stage by a Pap smear test (a painless procedure that most American and European women take for granted), Nicaraguan doctors have lacked the equipment and expertise to perform this simple test. In August 1994, an American pathologist, as part of a PFP mission, went to this country hauling three crates of equipment donated by corporations such as Eli Lilly, 3M, Johnson & Johnson, Medtronics, and Hewlett-Packard. Within a few weeks, this physician taught the local doctors to perform Pap smears, and he left his own personal microscope behind as a gift.

In the United States, angioplasty is a routine procedure for certain cardiac problems—but it had never been attempted in

Palestine. The doctors who went there found a bright young Palestinian cardiologist who was considered an excellent candidate to learn the procedure. The organization brought him to Norfolk to study with a top angioplasty specialist. When the young doctor was finished with his training, his mentor, who happened to be Jewish, accompanied him to Palestine to observe and assist him with his first attempt at the procedure.

Contributing to PFP is a "good investment," says Charles Horton. "Last year we delivered more than four million dollars' worth of medical equipment, antibiotics, and physicians' services, which are always donated freely, and we spent less than two hundred thousand for all of our operating expenses."

Charles Horton grew up in the "barefoot Ozark Mountains of Missouri." It was as a child there that he observed the kindness and generosity his parents offered freely to their friends and neighbors. His decision to enter medicine was simple, he says. Like most people who become doctors, he'd always wanted to work in a caring profession and help other people. "I don't recall any conversion on the road to Damascus with a bright light like Saul had," he says. "But recognizing our common humanity and the need to express compassion was just something that I grew up with. My parents never sat down and taught me values, they just lived them."

Horton and Physicians for Peace have won many awards and commendations for their altruism, including the highest award given to civilians in Jordan, the Independence Order First Class, which King Hussein presented to them in the capital city of Anman. PFP's success in forging friendships, particularly in the Middle East, was recognized by President Clinton when he invited Horton to attend the signing of the 1993 Peace Accord at the White House. While he considers these accolades an honor, Horton is adamant in his belief that the real value of his work is in the missions themselves, regardless of any hoopla that attends them. "As we receive foreign medical, dental, and nursing scholars and introduce them to our hometown churches, synagogues, mosques, and civic clubs, we reinforce the fact that there are good people from all parts of the world," he has written. "As we reduce the philosophical distances between countries by working together, friendships are stimulated, correspondence and communications are expanded, misunderstandings are reduced, and peace becomes a realistic goal."

Horton is showing me the PFP's new fund-raising brochure. On the front page is a simple headline: "What happens when you put the world's oldest enemies together in one small room, with a half-dozen very sharp knives?" He turns the page: "They use them," reads a caption. Below the words is a photograph showing doctors and nurses, of all races and ethnic groups, in the midst of surgery.

Unlike doctors in the PFP, Richard Andrews doesn't need to travel far to practice "Third World medicine." In the second-poorest county in Virginia, his small clinic in Nassawadox (the name is from a Native American word meaning "between two waters") provides the only medical care for poor local residents and migrant farmworkers, who pour into the area from Central and South America during the spring and summer months. Although trained in family practice, this rural doctor is just as likely to be working as a pediatrician, obstetrician, dermatologist, infectious disease specialist, dentist, psychologist, or librarian.

On any given day, this energetic, fortyish physician, who describes himself as "a bit of a workaholic," is running between the five small clinics funded by a community health organization. The staff includes nurses, nurse practitioners, social workers, and a driver for the van, but Richard is the only doctor. He's busy throughout the year; in the peak summer months, he will care for thirty to sixty patients a day. Setting broken bones, bandaging wounds, delivering babies, offering medical advice, and treating all kinds of chronic illnesses, tuberculosis, AIDS, and leprosy among them, are just part of his work here. His clinics collect used clothing, stock canned goods in a community food pantry, and offer counseling for staying healthy and for controlling domestic violence.

Considering himself politically and medically progressive, Richard is convinced that the healthcare of his community must encompass more than just traditional medical treatment. "Of course, I'm concerned about the health of my individual patients, but everything takes place in a context. Family medical practice needs to be holistic and take into account all aspects of a person's life," he tells me. Richard uses as an example unemployment and poverty, which have been shown to contribute to hypertension, which, in turn, can cause heart disease. These social problems are also related to substance abuse, domestic violence, and despair. Seeing a patient in an examining room is only part of what healing is about. In this view, education and literacy, and fostering feelings of community, are as important to health as are clean water and access to antibiotics.

"Illiteracy is a major problem in the health of many communities, and it's surprisingly high for an affluent country like ours," Richard tells me as we talk in the Nassawadox Free Library, which he established in 1993. Friends told him that the name he'd chosen sounded "way too sixtyish," but he stuck with it anyway. He wanted people to know that everyone could come here and freely use the books.

The library idea was born six years ago. It came to Richard as he was walking past his clinic and saw a vacant store—a tiny, wood-framed building. "The 'For Rent' sign sparked me," he says. "It seemed that if I rented this space and put up a sign that said 'Library,' things would start to happen. People would donate books. Libraries are almost universally loved. All of the world's knowledge should be available to everyone."

The entire library is kept in one small room. It has handmade bookshelves, a table, five chairs, and a computer that keeps track of checkouts and returns. Richard is planning to rent another small building down the street for an annex that will have enough space for meetings and book discussion groups—a place for the community to come together and learn from and about one another. Until then, he'll have to wait to arrange such activities, because this little building is packed—there isn't room for another chair or bookshelf. The 18,000 volumes that have been donated since the library opened are neatly arranged on the shelves, and organized by the Library of Congress cataloguing system. "We try to have books on almost every topic," he says. "We keep track of the number of patrons, and our numbers increase every month."

A middle-aged black man is browsing the shelves. "Hey, Doc," he asks, "you got anything on sports?"

Richard helps him find that section as a woman enters. "How's your Spanish coming?" he asks her. Richard speaks fluent Spanish, a necessary part of his involvement with the migrant workers here. *"Bueno, bueno,"* she says laughing. She tells him that she's applied for a job and wants to use him as a reference. She's worked with him, as a driver for the vans that pick up migrant workers and deliver them to the clinics for health-care screenings. "No problem at all," he says. "I can't wait to let them know how great you are."

A graduate of the University of Connecticut Medical School with a residency at Georgetown University, Richard has taken a different path from that taken by the majority of his fellow students, many of whom maintain prosperous private practices. I tell Richard I want to understand why he has made the choices he has. He warns me I would be making a mistake to see what he is doing as purely altruistic. "Of course, I would like to help people, but if I didn't get off on what I'm doing it wouldn't be enough. Medicine to me has always been the perfect blend of science and working with people."

In Richard's philosophy, everyone has dignity and deserves to be treated with respect. All people should have access to the basic human needs of food, shelter, and education. This belief in the intrinsic nobility of every person was something that both his mother and father showed him, not by teaching it directly, but by living it every day.

Richard's family moved to Spain when he was eighteen months old. As he was growing up there, his friends included boys and girls from both the wealthiest and the poorest families. His mother was a teacher and his father was a petroleum chemist, a career civil servant working with the Navy. Richard saw that whether his father was talking to an admiral, a Nobel Prize winner, or a janitor, he treated them all exactly the same.

"We didn't grow up with any religious ideas," says Richard, but neither of his parents spoke disparagingly of religion, and all the kids in the family were free to find their own beliefs. "There was unconditional love and the full understanding that we would always be loved, and important parts of the family, whether we made big successes of our lives or not. That, I think, fits in with the idea that people have dignity no matter what their situation in life."

Richard finds his philosophical base not in the liturgy of religion, but in the U.S. Constitution. He believes that a vigorous democracy is the best and perhaps the only way of ensuring equality and dignity for everyone. To support those ideals,

Richard has decided to run as an independent for state delegate to the General Assembly for the 100th District. "I like the guy who's in," he says. "He's nice, bright, and I think he even has integrity. But he's an incumbent who has been in office for the past nineteen years. That has to feed a certain complacency. Open debate, open discussion, and vigorous participation are what keeps democracy breathing. Low-income people will always get the short end of the stick unless we all work to keep things moving forward, shaking things up a bit."[2]

Richard's niece Cary has come to visit him for a few weeks and he has recruited her to work on the computer. As I'm leaving, she has a question for him about how to enter some newly donated books. The man who had been looking for a book on sports needs more help in the Biography section. A woman enters with some paperwork for Richard to sign. He gives her a big hug and takes the files from her. It's Saturday morning, but the day is just beginning for this physician/librarian/political candidate. He has a lot to do: organize his campaign, make sure that a shipment of medical supplies has arrived, schedule infant inoculations for next week, and, as always, re-shelve returned books.

The sky has been overcast. It's starting to drizzle now, and before the day is over, the clouds will release one of their crop-drenching spring rains so common here on the Eastern Shore. A sputtering pickup truck pulls in next to me, kicking up the dust of the unpaved parking area. The back of the truck is full of rusty hoes and shovels, metal buckets, crab pots, and an ancient dog. The Latino man behind the wheel smiles and touches the brim of his dirty straw hat in greeting. Two small girls—maybe six and eight years old—jump from the cab, clutching books to their chests to keep them from getting wet, and race toward the door of the library. *"¡Buenos días!"* they yell to me. *"Buenos días,"* I call back. It is indeed a good day.

Like Charles Horton and Richard Andrews, Jack Powell is redefining and stretching his goals as he has come to understand his own part of the universal journey toward healing. In fact, this pediatrician has found that his career, even his whole life, has been changed by his response to a single letter from a little girl.

Jack is a physician and a lieutenant colonel serving at Wright-Patterson Air Force Base outside Dayton, Ohio. He's always had a wide range of interests, and after two decades of medical practice he was looking for ways to reduce the isolation of chronically ill children. "Did you ever wake up at three o'clock in the morning, feeling sick?" he asks me. "You look out the window, the world is dark and it feels like nobody's there. It's a very isolated feeling and one that sick kids deal with daily."

In the children's ward at Wright-Patterson, Jack has seen firsthand the effects of that loneliness. He's seen problems that sick children have in just being kids and relating to their peers without falling victim to the stigma and limitations of their illnesses. His very early interest in the Internet convinced him that this new technology had enormous potential to help children, especially those in hospitals, to communicate with others, to have a place to play, and to express themselves, all without leaving their sickbeds. He began to explore the possibilities.

An early conversation with the programmers at America Online put Jack in contact with a children's media writer and Internet consultant, Genevieve Kazdin, who lives in Cape Cod and whom he still has not met. At the time, the Internet was not easily accessible, and the World Wide Web was not yet up and running, but it was clear that this new technology was developing at a rapid pace, so Jack and Gen began to brainstorm via e-mail about the possibilities of installing computers in hospitals. "Children think of themselves as children first and sick children second. We wanted to give them opportunities to be just kids," he says.

As they tinkered with the idea, it quickly became clear that their biggest obstacle would be getting hardware. Sick children come from families of every economic stratum, and many couldn't be expected to have access to a computer. If Jack's and Gen's ideas were to be implemented, the hospital would have to provide the computers. Given the great scaling-down of health-care dollars, where would the equipment come from?

Several years passed as Jack and Gen continued to explore possibilities of grants or donations of computer equipment. Their lives were busy and they couldn't devote full-time attention to this idea. Then, three years ago, Jack received a letter from Alexis, an eleven-year-old girl with multiple medical problems, who had been in touch with Gen. Alexis had been given a Notebook computer by the Apple Computer Corporation and had recently been hospitalized for three weeks. She was writing to Jack not for herself, but for the other kids she'd met during her hospitalization. In her letter she told him how lonely it is in hospitals, which confirmed his own observations that this is a major problem for sick children. Many of the children whom Alexis had met in the hospital had been there longer than she had and were going to be there after she left. Some had very few visitors, and most never received cards or phone calls. She had found that she was happier when she could talk to other kids on chat lines or play games with them through her computer. But none of the other children could do that. She needed Jack's help. "Isn't there something that you can do to help my friends?" she wrote.

He was tremendously moved by this young girl's letter, not only by her articulate expressiveness but also by her determination to help others. After he'd put the letter into his briefcase, two peculiar events occurred simultaneously. First, he received an e-mail that was accidentally broadcast to the entire hospital. (The Air Force had just installed a new e-mail system, and personnel were still working out the bugs.) The message, which was intended for only a few people in the information system division, described a program to recycle surplus computers as the military upgraded their equipment. In a curious coincidence, Jack's next appointment was unexpectedly canceled. Since his office was only a few blocks from the warehouse where this surplus equipment was being stored, and now that he had an hour free, he walked over there. He was stunned by what he saw: rows upon rows of IBM-compatible computers stacked to the ceiling in a building half the size of a football field. They were old 286 and 386 models that had been replaced by newer, faster ones. "The hardware problem was solved right then," he says.

"Imagine the idea of taking taxpayer-owned computers and shipping them off to children's hospitals. Still, I knew that it would take time to work through all the permissions and paperwork to have it happen," he says. Expecting only snafus and roadblocks, Jack was overwhelmed by the effort the Air Force and other governmental agencies made in getting these discarded computers to children's hospitals. "People in the government were quite excited to be able to help. Every single bureaucrat, instead of becoming an obstacle, became a helper. They saw that they could do something to help kids. I learned just how much people in government do care. It was a huge network of ordinary people—from enlisted clerks to the surgeon general of the Air Force—with an extraordinary opportunity to be kind." The paperwork went through with record speed, and "First Team" was up and running less than a year after Jack's initial request.

Once people learned about the project, Jack had no lack of volunteers. A crew of enlisted personnel and officers offered to help. In their spare time, these men and women—some of them experts with computers, and others medical technicians, doctors, and nurses struggling to learn how to use their own home PCs— put together a website called PlanIt Hospital, which offered children a variety of activities, a means of communication, and a way to offer feedback to hospitals and doctors about improving their care.[3] About one-third of the site is "hidden," because Jack and the others know how kids like to go to secret places, hacking into areas that seem off-limits. Their intuition is confirmed by data that show that these areas are the most well-traveled parts of the website. The many hours of work donated by volunteers, the generosity of Prodigy in providing on-line time, and the recycling of abandoned computers have kept the costs of this marvelous program under $11,000.

For the past three years, every minute of Jack's free time has been devoted to the First Team project, and his commitment to it has changed his plans about his professional future. Because of the time he's given to the project, he deferred taking the advanced courses necessary for promotion to colonel, and without that promotion he will be required to retire from the Air Force next year with twenty years of active service, instead of the thirty that he had originally planned on. This, he points out, is not punishment from the Air Force—in fact they have been extremely supportive of his project—but simply the result of opting for a different career path.

"I'm constantly reminded that in a person's life there are times when decisions have to be made that will color the rest of your life for good or for bad," he says. "This decision made itself. I try to make choices on the basis of which ones will help me sleep better at night, and I simply could not turn my back on Alexis. I've never met her and I probably never will. But I was haunted by her letter and thought 'There but for the grace of God goes any one of us.' When this child spoke out, made a direct request, on the behalf of other children, I was trapped by compassion. She asked me that question, 'Can you help?' and by a series of coincidences, at ten-thirty on the morning that I read her letter, I could answer, 'Yes, I sure can.' No matter what the ultimate outcome, I'll always know that I gave it my best shot."

Jack fully understands that electronic communication will never, and should never, replace face-to-face contact, but he also knows that this technology can provide a level playing field for chronically ill children and those with disabilities. In cyberspace, sharing ideas and the creative use of resources are more important than how fast you can run or how well you can throw a ball. It's a new reality for disabled and sick children. "Children know that it's a vast world out there, and sometimes it seems that this world doesn't know or care that they're here. But they can send a message out to the unknown—like shooting an arrow into space—and someone responds, affirming that they exist. It has a powerful effect," he says.

So much of the debate about technology has centered on its dangers, its tendency to replace human contact, and its dissemination of the prosaic and smutty that it is easy to lose sight of the amazing opportunities it offers. Jack believes that "children now and in the future are going to be connected electronically. They are going to build their society by learning to work together for common goals. Technology determines that geography is no longer a problem—children all over the world can communicate. Because messages can be left on message boards, time won't be a problem either. These are barriers that we've faced but that these children don't have to."

As I log on and sort through the junk e-mail that has accumu-lated, I'm struck by how the virtual world seems no different than real life. All these offers to sell me something reflect the same emphasis on commercialism that I find jamming my regu-lar mailbox in front of my house. Several of these unsolicited messages invite me to visit pornographic websites. I immediately delete those and wonder what rocket scientist put together this mailing list that could possibly include me, a middle-aged femi-nist woman, as part of this particular "target market." Although I've discovered a great deal of useful information on a variety of subjects on the Internet, most of what I find in the virtual world seems benign, neither good nor bad, though some items, such as the four hundred haikus about the lunch-meat Spam, are quite amusing. I agree with Jack when he says, "Technology is nothing more than an opportunity—it can be used or misused. Every-thing depends upon what people do with it."

The First Team website is brimming with interactive oppor-tunities for kids of all ages. They can read or download classic books by H. G. Wells, Jules Verne, and Edgar Rice Burroughs; read uplifting folk tales from every continent and culture; respond to trivia questions; engage in more serious discussions about life; and contribute to group poems where different chil-dren each add a line. This site contains many creative ways in which children can interact and play games together. At this moment, there is a vigorous ongoing debate concerning the hypothetical question of whether the Starship *Enterprise* (from *Star Trek*) or an Imperial Star Destroyer (from *Star Wars*) would prevail if they were to engage in a space battle. The long thread of responses contains everything from "The Enterprise would win 'cause it's huge, dude," to highly technical explanations about the clear superiority of turboblasters, photon torpedoes, ion cannons, and Tie fighters in defense of the Imperial ship. In an Art Gallery area, kids can draw their own pictures, set them in exotic frames, and hang them on a virtual museum wall. The participation of many sick children is clear from the titles of some of the work here: "The Lab," "Nurse," "I Get a Visitor," "Coming to the Emergency Room," and "Hospital." I am particularly taken with a vivid drawing by a six-year-old named Missy. It is a self-portrait that invites other children to come and talk to her. She has drawn herself with an enormous smile and has called it: "Missy Says Hello to the World."

All three of these doctors are wonderful examples of how ordinary grace shows itself as a bright light in the midst of potential darkness. Charles Horton and Physicians for Peace operate in a world of turmoil, violence, and hatred. The underlying philosophy of this organization—the very reason for its existence—is to make peace in war-torn countries by reducing hatred through friendship and shared knowledge. Charles Horton and the others have taken strife and animosity and rendered them into sharing and compassion.

Richard Andrews works in an environment of great economic distress and illness—a reflection of the classism that exists in our own nation. Here in the United States, this rural doctor treats cases of leprosy and malnutrition not unlike those seen throughout the Third World. Again, we see the power of grace—the healing, the sharing of knowledge through books— even in the midst of poverty and illiteracy.

The ordinary grace illuminated by Jack Powell spreads compassion through the ineffable and complicated world of cyberspace, and brings friendship and play to isolated children. Technology is often criticized for its coldness and lack of humanity; as just one more reason that there is such lack of grace in the world. We hear people say, "Computers will be our downfall. They'll be no more face-to-face relationships. They're turning us into robots." The truth is that technology in itself is neither good nor bad in a moral sense. Its value has only to do with how we put it to use. Jack Powell shows us that caring has a place even in the virtual world.

These three examples of ordinary grace show how clearly goodness and compassion can emerge out of difficult, troubled places where war, poverty, and moral uncertainty abound. The fact is that grace exists everywhere—even in the most despairing circumstances. Why is it that we think we don't have choices about what to focus on—what we choose to tune in to? We certainly understand that we have these choices in other parts of our life.

At this moment, you are reading this book. You have made a *choice* to focus on these words printed on these physical pages in front of you. In doing so, you are choosing to ignore other sources of information. For example, right now you are also surrounded by electromagnetic radiation. If you don't believe me, just turn on a radio or television—every radio and TV broadcast in the world is present in the room with you. Turn the channels and you will see that some signals are stronger than others. With some you will have to adjust your receiver to get a clear signal; others are immediately and distinctly discernible. The signals that you can now hear or see were there, surrounding you, before you elected to attend to them, before you hit the "on" button. You did not initiate them, but you became conscious of them by making a choice to tune in to them.

Every day we make choices about these kinds of seemingly inconsequential things, like what television or radio program we will turn on. Think of all the others: which restaurant we will go to, what movie we want to see, whether we will mow the lawn or watch a baseball game on television. Does it make sense that we should focus our attention on the banal choices in our lives and not on the decisions about how our spirit will live?

Grace is always present; it surrounds us at every moment of every day in profoundly moving experiences and in small, almost imperceptible ways. Grace is present in straw huts where a child's cleft palate is being surgically repaired, in a small clinic where a young mother is learning how to care for her infant, and on the screens of computers where lonely children call out to one another. Grace doesn't just live in the blessed sounds emanating from great cathedrals and holy ashrams—the sacred is all around us. Listen. Open your eyes.

8.

The Dark Side

This thing of darkness I acknowledge mine.

—William Shakespeare, *The Tempest*

Every author dreams of the day when his or her book will go to auction, when several major publishing houses will attempt to outbid one another for the opportunity to publish it. An auction represents an author's best chance to earn a great deal of money, since it can drive up the amount of the publisher's advance.

Recently, a highly regarded literary agent, while shopping a new thriller by one of her clients, misrepresented the number of publishers bidding on it. After the auction had gone several rounds, all but one of them had dropped out, but the agent decided not to say so. Despite the fact that the one remaining publisher had already made a preemptive bid of $350,000 for the novel, and an additional offer of $500,000 for two more books, she maintained her bluff and kept on with the auction. Unfortunately for the agent, the publisher discovered her deception and canceled its offer, which left her to try to salvage an earlier, lower bid.

To her credit, the agent recognized her behavior as unethical, accepted full responsibility for it, and hoped that this one mistake would not overshadow a decade of honest work. What is most interesting is how she described the decision to act outside her usual moral standards. Her dishonesty, she said in an interview, emerged in the "heat of battle" and "from a part of me that I didn't know existed before."[1] Without going into the matter too deeply, perhaps without even knowing it, this literary agent aptly described her "shadow."

As each of us grows older and journeys down the long road of socialization, we begin to understand which of our qualities are rewarded by society and which are not. Human beings have a deep need to be accepted by their parents and peers. We are a helpless species at birth—the most helpless of animals, in fact—and we remain so for a long time. We are born into the world with the instinctive knowledge that we would perish if we were not accepted by our caretakers, and so we give ourselves over to learning how to behave from our families, religions, teachers, and the culture at large. We *need* to be assimilated into the tribe. Very quickly we integrate the "positive" traits—those that we know will be acceptable—into the face that we show to the rest of the world. The socialization of the species is accomplished by the development of these aspects of our personality, which psychologist Carl Jung called the "persona."

The word *persona* comes from the Latin name for the masks that actors in the ancient world wore to portray certain characters in the theater. We can think of the persona as the appearance we choose to show other people, and as the many different roles we play in our lives. The way we dress, the language we use, and the modes of behavior we use at home or at work are all parts of our persona. Although it allows us to believe that we are unique, Jung observed that the persona "feigns individuality": this self that we present is, in fact, only a convenient fiction about who we are. "Fundamentally, the persona is nothing real: It is a compromise between the individual and society as to what a man should appear to be," he wrote.[2]

The persona plays a major role in our psychological and social lives, and represents a part of us—but only a part. Problems begin when we identify too strongly with the mask that we show to the world, and when we believe that it is an honest and exact representation of everything within us. It is easy to think that all we are is the face we show to others, but that is not true.

All the rejected aspects of our personality form another sub-personality, which Jung called the "shadow." This repression is both unconscious and automatic, and in the Western world, which has been influenced heavily by Judeo-Christian values, it almost always includes our natural sexual and aggressive tendencies. So, too, do we repress greed, lust, jealousy, selfishness—

anything that we consider unacceptable. Jung referred to the shadow as "the thing one has no wish to be." The Jungian analyst and writer Marion Woodman observed that "the shadow can be anything in our 'holier than thou' attitudes that we think that we're not."[3]

A full discussion of the human shadow could fill many books, but four major points bear mentioning here. First, in addition to all the negative aspects of our character, we may also repress positive human characteristics—creativity, spontaneity, tolerance, compassion—depending on the values we've grown up with. For example, if your family taught you that "it's a dog-eat-dog world," that you have to protect your interests because no one else will, you might find your instinct for trust stifled, banished to a psychic underworld. It's important to remember that there is gold in the shadow as well as darkness. The shadow contains all of the unlived life, all the things that we think we are not, whether they're positive or negative.

Second, just because we have repressed certain traits does not mean that they are gone forever. In fact, although the shadow is unconscious, it often offers conscious clues about its contents. Recognizing the shadow is not difficult if we are willing to reflect honestly on our feelings and behaviors. Although many people avoid such introspection because of the terror involved in looking into our own dark nature, it is only through honest self-evaluation that we discover our authentic Self and can live with wisdom and meaning.

For those willing to make the journey, the path to the shadow can be seen in several ways: (1) the projection of our own psyche onto others through exaggerated, often immediate judgments that say more about us than the targets of our criticism ("Disgusting. Look at how short that woman's dress is"); (2) feedback from others, especially when we hear the same thing from many different sources ("Nancy and I both feel you are not being truthful with us"); (3) inadvertent and impulsive actions, humor, and "slips of the tongue" ("I never meant to say that—I was only kidding"); (4) situations in which we feel shame; and (5) our dreams, fantasies, and creative endeavors.[4]

Third, the less we understand our inner life, the more likely the cast-off attributes in our unconscious are to express themselves when we least expect it. Remember the story of the literary agent at the beginning of this chapter? She was someone who had always operated under appropriate professional and ethical standards, but who fell under the influence of her own greedy shadow in the middle of a major book deal. She said that the decision to act immorally came from "a part of me that I didn't know existed before." If you have ever said, "I don't know what came over me. I just wasn't myself," then you understand the power of the shadow.

Fourth, the more inflated and out of balance someone's persona is, the more forcefully the shadow bursts forth from the unconscious. "The brighter the light, the darker the shadow" is a good way to think of this phenomenon. The Greek philosopher Heraclitus described this process as *enantiodromia*—a mouthful of a word that simply means "running counter to" or "opposite."

Things that are out of balance in one direction tend to create an opposing force equally out of balance in the other direction.

Stories about elected officials, celebrities, and religious leaders whose outer personae belie dark shadows and who experience a resulting fall from grace fill the news. The sting is always sharpest when we discover the dark side of a person from whom we expect moral, ethical, and spiritual integrity. So many of our heroes end up having feet of clay. Watergate, Iran-contra, the Clarence Thomas hearings, Travelgate, President Clinton and Monica Lewinsky—a week doesn't go by when some national figure isn't being investigated for an immoral or illegal act. Jim Bakker, televangelist and preacher, who interprets the Holy Bible and lets his congregants know, in no uncertain terms, how they are to live, goes to jail for bilking his contributors out of millions of dollars. Jimmy Swaggart, bellowing from the pulpit about morals and values and how most of us are sinners, is caught with a prostitute by a police sting operation. The Catholic Church pays retribution to men who were sexually abused by priests when they were adolescent boys. Lawsuits are brought against Swami Rama, the spiritual leader of a yoga institute, for sexual misconduct. Best-selling author and Tibetan Buddhist teacher Sogyal Rinpoche is charged with inducing female students to have sexual intercourse with him as part of their search for "enlightenment." Complaints against him also include assault and battery. Episcopal bishop Edward Chalfant, of Maine, takes a one-year disciplinary leave of absence after admitting to an extramarital affair.[5]

The task for each of us in struggling to live moral lives is in learning to "hold the tension of the opposites." This means neither acting out our dark energies nor repressing them entirely into the unconscious. In speaking of the compensating powers of the persona and the shadow, Jungian analyst and writer Anthony Stevens observes: "As can be predicted from its mode of development, the shadow complex possesses qualities opposite of those manifested in the persona. Consequently, these two aspects of the personality complement and counterbalance each other, the shadow compensating for the pretensions of the persona, the persona compensating for the antisocial propensities of the shadow."[6]

It is this dialectic, this holding of the tension between the good and evil qualities in our awareness, that allows us to move toward higher levels of consciousness, individuation, and enlightenment. This mindfulness acts as a fulcrum and keeps the natural self-regulating mechanisms of the psyche in balance. It takes considerable psychic energy to repress certain parts of ourselves, and by bringing those aspects to awareness, by becoming conscious of our own true humanity with all its wrinkles and warts, we liberate a potent energy from the shadow. At the same time, we avoid the inflation that comes with believing that we are only good. When we deny that we are capable of evil ourselves, we deprive ourselves of any real chance to understand the evil of others. Rumi, with his typical economy of language, understands this point when he says, "If thou hast not seen the devil, look at thine own self."[7]

Just as we each have a personal shadow and our collective unconscious casts its own long specter, life itself has its dark side. Illness, death, accidents, and violence can all be seen as part of the natural shadow of the world. But even in life's bleakest moments, ordinary grace can flourish and pull light from the darkness, hope from despair, and life from death itself. The story that follows is a beautiful example of such flourishing—of the positive aspects of the shadow coming to light because of a devastating loss. The great poet Kahlil Gibran reflected on how even the most bottomless sorrow can be transformed into joy and a celebration of life when he wrote:

> *Your joy is your sorrow unmasked . . .*
> *The deeper that sorrow carves into your being*
> *the more joy you can contain.*[8]

Amy Barzach says that her son Jonathan had "old eyes." Even on the day he was born, he seemed to look out onto the world with a deep wisdom and a quiet understanding. Still, he was a happy, healthy baby, always smiling, who loved to be held by his mother and father and tickled by his three-year-old brother Daniel.

At four and half months, Jonathan suddenly began to have problems holding his head up—it was as if his neck could no longer bear the weight. His parents, Amy and Peter Barzach, immediately took him to their pediatrician. Amy remembers her panic on that day: "There was a phone call from the pediatric neurologist on the answering machine before we even got home from that appointment. He wanted to see Jonathan first thing in the morning."

Medical tests over the next six weeks confirmed their pediatrician's initial and devastating impression. Jonathan had spinal muscular atrophy, an inherited nerve disease that causes wasting and increasing weakness of the muscles, and that would eventually make it difficult, or impossible, for him to eat or breathe. Even worse, Jonathan had a particularly virulent and progressive form of the disease. So began four months of doctors, hospitals, medicine, and many tears.

Peter and Amy, who live in West Hartford, Connecticut, are used to making things happen. "Give us an impossible task," Peter tells me, "and we'll find answers." Both had learned to overcome adversity in their own lives. Peter and his family emigrated from Russia to Israel when he was eleven years old. At that time, the Communist government considered all emigrating Jews to be "traitors," and withdrew their citizenship. Those leaving for Israel were held in particular contempt since their new country was considered an enemy of Russia's allies in the Middle East. Peter's father was a professional athlete, his mother a high-ranking engineer who built oil refineries. They had lived a comfortable life in Russia, but they were forced to leave all their property and money behind. In 1973, the couple left for Israel with two young sons, a couple of suitcases full of clothes, and very little money. Peter was the only one in the family who spoke any English—he had studied it in the fifth grade—and he became their "mouthpiece." Two years later, the Barzachs came to the United States and settled in Hartford, where they built a life from scratch. Peter discovered that he had a talent for both finance and computers. He earned a degree in business from Trinity College in Hartford and took a high-level job as a business manager for international programs at a Hartford aerospace technology company. His job required him to live in Moscow for six months of the year. As an adult, he found himself sitting across the bargaining table and negotiating multimillion-dollar business contracts with the same former Communist leaders who had, years earlier, declared his family traitors.

Amy describes herself as having been a "painfully shy" girl. She developed scoliosis just as she entered high school. Wearing a back brace she named "Matilda," she felt acute embarrassment at exactly the time when kids feel the greatest urge to fit in with their peers. Amy asked her mother to buy every color turtleneck she could find, so she could hide her infirmity from her classmates, and she would wear them even in hot summer weather. In college, she wanted to major in education but decided against it because she couldn't face speaking in front of a group of students. After graduation, she registered for a training session in public speaking. It was wonderful. For the first time she began to feel greater self-confidence. She then went into a line of work that would force her not to be shy and to present her views in front of other people. She learned a great deal from these experiences, although they were painful. She began to deliberately put herself into situations that would help her to overcome her fear of receiving any kind of attention. After the birth of her first child, Daniel, she decided to reduce her work as the vice-president of marketing for The Hutensky Group—a management firm for shopping centers—to part-time. She also began to work as a consultant and offered training and marketing seminars throughout the region. She was conducting workshops, speaking in front of groups of people, expressing her own opinions about marketing, and loving it.

In spite of their considerable talents for overcoming difficult odds and making things happen, Amy and Peter could do nothing to help Jonathan. "We were fighting every day to find answers for this disease," Peter says. He spoke with doctors in the United States, in Russia, and all over the world. Amy searched through hundreds of medical journals and read everything she could find about the disease. They consulted experts. They requested second and third opinions. They investigated all kinds of alternative therapies. Nothing they did could stop the progress of Jonathan's disease. It became clear that their beloved son was going to die.

During the last few months of his life, Jonathan was hospitalized constantly, and the family's friends and co-workers rallied around them to help whenever they could. One friend developed a computerized schedule of things that could be done for the Barzachs. Friends arranged to take Daniel to dinner, movies, and outings so that he could get away from the hospital. Several mothers of Daniel's nursery-schoolmates made lunches for him and coordinated picking him up after school. Friends cooked gourmet dinners for Peter and Amy to eat on the rare nights when they would come home from the hospital to get a few hours of sleep. Their rabbi, James Rosen of Beth El, cut short a vacation in New York to return and comfort them. When it was clear that Jonathan was about to die, Amy called a Borders bookstore to find children's titles about grief and mourning that might help Daniel through the death of his brother. The Borders employee who helped her decided on his own to send Jonathan a Paddington Bear and a card showing a child slaying a dragon.

The Barzachs knew that time was running out and that every day, every moment, with Jonathan was precious. Daniel thought that his little brother would feel happy if he could see dolphins and, in particular, beluga whales, the white and graceful animals that he especially loved. A special trip to the Mystic Aquarium for a private look at these peaceful creatures was arranged. Daniel was right. Jonathan smiled and watched with great interest. A few days later, on January 5, 1995, Jonathan died. He was nine months old.

As Jonathan was dying, Amy and Peter worked with a hospice counselor who helped them through their grief. "She had a magical presence," Amy says. "She would walk into the room and put her hands on Jonathan's shoulders and his heart rate would return to normal. She had such a physically calming effect. She helped us, too. When Jonathan was sick, I felt that everything I was good at was useless. Who cares if you can manage a project, which is what I do for my job? Who cares if you can teach people? What good are any of those skills?" The hospice counselor told them that someday they would find a way to use those skills to do something that would have great meaning and give a lasting legacy to Jonathan's short life. The Barzachs had donated Jonathan's organs and were comforted to be able to help other children with this gift, but they knew that there would have to be something more. "She never gave answers but she asked the right questions," Amy says of the counselor. "Still, I couldn't imagine what could possibly have enough meaning."

One night, a few weeks after Jonathan's death, the Barzachs went to dinner and passed by a fence company that was displaying a huge wooden boat with swings and slides—a great piece of playground equipment. They talked about buying it and donating it to Daniel's school in memory of Jonathan. The next day they got up at five in the morning and drove back to the wooden boat. As they climbed all over it, they realized that if Jonathan had lived he would never have been able to play on it. He would have been crippled by his disease, confined to a wheelchair. Amy remembered taking Daniel and Jonathan to a park and seeing a little girl sitting off to the side in a wheelchair, unable to play with the other kids. The girl had sat and watched the other children, her chin quivering, on the verge of tears.

During Jonathan's illness, Amy and Peter had met a five-year-old girl, Carissa, at the hospital. She had a milder form of spinal muscular atrophy, the same disease that was killing their son, and used a wheelchair. Now they thought about her and what could be done so that she could play alongside her able-bodied friends.

They decided to build a special playground in such a way that all children, regardless of any special physical challenges, could play together. It would be a permanent legacy of Jonathan's short life. They began to visit dozens of playgrounds and tested each piece of equipment to see if it could be used by disabled children. Even little Daniel was becoming an expert. "Carissa couldn't get up there," he'd tell them.

They discovered that there were few models on which to base their design. Even playgrounds built to Americans with Disabilities Act standards are generally only twenty to twenty-five percent accessible for children in wheelchairs. "If Jonathan had grown up, we wouldn't have wanted him to be a loner," Peter says. "We didn't want to build a playground only for kids in wheelchairs, but a place where those children could play alongside and have as much fun as their friends." The playground that was emerging in their minds would be more than just wheelchair-accessible. It would be wheelchair-*friendly.*

Just as the hospice counselor had predicted, Peter and Amy were beginning to use their considerable organizational, research, and management skills to develop the initial idea for "Jonathan's Dream."

In the fall of 1995, Amy and Peter arranged to meet with two hundred children, half of whom had special needs, for "Dreaming and Design Parties." Using Legos, modeling clay, tongue depressors, crayons, and whatever else was available, these kids showed the Barzachs what they wanted. A company in the Hartford area donated the drawing and design materials, another delivered pizza and soda, another sent people to take photographs of the children's creations. The designs included tree-houses, glider boats, limousines, swings, trains, overhead ropes, and raised sandboxes. Remembering the last good time he had spent with his little brother, Daniel presented his own idea—a baby beluga whale slide. The children's plans were turned over to a nationally respected playground architect, Christopher Clews of Learning Structures, who translated them into workable architectural designs. The place would be truly intergenerational, with benches and cool areas where relatives and other adults could sit comfortably and talk while watching the children.

Peter established a budget and a management approach for the project. It would be an expensive undertaking, especially given the wood-polymer playground surface required to make it truly wheelchair-friendly. The previously "painfully shy" Amy began to talk to various civic groups about the idea, in hopes of getting a dozen or so volunteers to help. Within months of one of her talks, sixty-two Rotary groups in Connecticut and southern Massachusetts had taken on Jonathan's Dream as an official project. An artist donated the drawing for a logo showing two children—one in a wheelchair, the other standing alongside—and an older person, thus emphasizing the intergenerational and inclusive philosophy behind the playground. All three figures are reaching for stars. Another person who heard about the playground, and who owned a printing company, said the project would need proper stationery if fund-raising was being planned; everything about it had to show that it was legitimate and worthy of donations. After learning what Jonathan's Dream was about, the print-shop employees came in after office hours to run the letterhead on their own time.

The Greater Hartford Jewish Community Center dedicated a parcel of its own land for this public playground. More than $11,000 was raised from over four hundred individuals and clubs. Then a $35,000 grant from the Andre Lacroix Fund at the Hartford Foundation for Public Giving and a $10,000 donation from Paul Newman and Newman's Own Charities kicked things into high gear. More than $50,000 worth of tools, materials, and equipment was donated by area companies. Professionals volunteered their expertise in zoning, planning, and construction. Peter's co-workers in Russia took up collections, and men and women who earned the equivalent of less than $300 a month donated as much as $100 each. Support poured in from the entire West Hartford community and beyond: Mobil Oil Company, Hasbro, St. Thomas Seminary, the United Way, Catholic Family Services, the Capital Region Council of Churches, Easter Seals, the National Council of Jewish Women, the West Hartford Junior Women's Club, and many more. From large monetary grants to small acts of generosity, Jonathan's tragically brief life and what his family was trying to do to remember him spurred people to act from their hearts. A reporter who had interviewed Amy, and who was about to be married, asked that her wedding guests make contributions to Jonathan's Dream instead of giving her presents.

As at an old-fashioned barn raising, hundreds of volunteers from throughout the area converged on the site for the playground on October 9, 1996. Students, secretaries, dentists, and homemakers worked under the direction of construction professionals. Some pounded nails and sawed boards, others made sandwiches and poured cold drinks for the crews. "It was amazing," Amy says. "We had corporate executives working side-by-side with alternative-to-incarceration kids who were doing community service instead of going to jail. The kids said things like, 'People seem to respect us here,' and the executives said, 'I didn't know those kids could be so great.' " In just a little more than a year after the initial planning, the Barzachs and their network of supporters had made the dream a reality.

Peter has a new job now. He works at an office twenty minutes from home and is delighted not to have to spend months away from his family. On January 2, 1997, the Barzachs celebrated the one-year birthday of their daughter Alyssa, a healthy and beautiful baby. People have come from all over the world to study the design elements of Jonathan's Dream—there is no place else like it in the world. Not only is the playground wheelchair-friendly, but it's good for the environment. The material used for the wood-polymer surface is made from recycled plastic bags, shrink-wrap, and waste wood. It is safe and splinter-free, so the children can crawl and sit on it. Many of those visiting and researching this unique site have taken ideas back to their own communities to create similar playgrounds.[9]

On a cold late-January day, Amy takes me to see Jonathan's Dream. We don't expect to see too many children, but we are happily surprised. More than a dozen kids are there, bundled up in heavy coats and gloves, their parents stamping their feet to stay warm. There are musical wind chimes, bright banners and signs, tube phones, and tic-tac-toe games. The colorful pixel wall, where kids can create their own pictures, stands out in stark relief against the gray sky and brown leafless trees on this winter day. I see the treehouse that Carissa, the little girl in the wheelchair, and an able-bodied eight-year-old, Vanessa, had designed together. On it is a little sign: "Carissa & Vanessa's Tree House."

I am moved by how the Barzachs transformed their grief into such an extraordinary place, bringing light and life from the darkest shadow that any parent could experience. I am comforted by the goodness of the people and organizations that helped them realize their dream, a community that came together in honor of a baby whose memory will live on in a place where all children can play. And I wept as I watched a little boy laughing and slipping down the baby beluga whale slide—Daniel's soulful contribution to the memory of his little brother.

We come into life expecting loss. We begin with loss—separated from our mother's protective heartbeat, from the security of her womb, and from our sense of oneness with everything—as we are plunged into an unfamiliar and uncertain world. Life's *expected* losses carry a potent mythology—an acceptable story. We hope that, if everything goes according to plan, we will live to a ripe old age. We anticipate that we will outlive our parents and have to say good-bye to them; after all, most are twenty or more years older than we are. If we are wise, we understand that everything is

impermanent and that during our lives we will lose everything—
our looks, our intelligence, our possessions, our careers, our relationships—as we move down the path to our own inviolate
mortality. It is as the poet Rainer Maria Rilke wrote: "So we live,
forever saying farewell."[10] But we don't expect the death of our
child. It shatters our innocence and causes most people to rage at
the heavens, "Why me? Why have you forsaken me?" The death of
a child violates our ideas about life's plan. Perhaps that is why this
particular sorrow is considered by psychologists to be the single
most stressful and difficult life event that we can ever encounter.

The word *grief* comes from the Latin *gravis,* meaning "to bear."
Gravis is also the root of the word *gravity,* which aptly describes
the heaviness and depth of the wrenching pain left with the
Barzach family by Jonathan's death. Grief seems to have a singu-
lar power to bring out the dark side of people. Significant losses
can cause us to feel so out of control about life that we refuse to
trust others, to believe in God or in life itself. Reeling and spin-
ning through the shadowy underworld of sorrow causes many
people to become bitter, disenchanted, and—worst of all—
hard-hearted, closed emotionally and spiritually to the light of
hope. Think of people you know who have closed down after a
loss: the friend who will never love again because he was
betrayed; the relative who refuses to associate with the family
because of a past hurt; the person who holds everyone at a distance because he or she has suffered great sorrow.

We often describe grief as "being brokenhearted," and it is an
accurate image. But it is precisely this *broken-ness* that creates new

spaces for light and love to enter. Ancient alchemists gave us a metaphor to describe this potential for transformation. In changing a base metal, lead, into a splendid one, gold, they understood that the first step had to be the *nigredo,* or "black phase," in which everything is melted down, broken into its elemental parts, before anything could be re-created. This is like the loss that plunges us from the everyday reality of our comfortable, familiar lives into the shadowy underworld of sorrow—what St. John of the Cross called "the dark night of the soul." It is a moment that opens us to ordinary grace and allows us to put things back together differently, as the Barzachs have done.

Look at all the smaller stories within this story. Think about the many ways that Jonathan's Dream pulled a community of people together. Look at how these ordinary people—of all different ages, occupations, races, faiths—joined to create a new future in which children of all abilities could play together. A stunning web of interconnectedness and grace spiraled out from the loss of this little boy. From the Borders clerk who took it upon himself to send a card and stuffed bear to a sick baby, to the professionals who donated their time, energy, and talent to bring light and fulfillment to what started as a wish from a broken heart. Peter and Amy Barzach took the high road. They knew that nothing could bring their beloved son back to them, but that they could nevertheless transform their anguish into kindness and concern for other children. And just as their hospice counselor had predicted, they used their talents and abilities as the tools to make this happen. Their devastating loss signaled a decision to embrace life, not to retreat or withdraw into their pain, and initiated a majestic call to celebrate and honor the spirit of their tiny Jonathan. At the moment of their decision, grace flowed like a river.

Ordinary grace helps us understand that God and Spirit are present in the shadows as well as the light. The German Christian mystic Meister Eckhart must have agreed, for he wrote, "God shines in the darkness where every now and then we get a glimpse of Him. More often, God is where His light is least apparent."

9.

What I've Learned
About Ordinary Grace

Whatever there is of God and goodness in the universe,

it must work itself out and express itself through us.

We cannot stand aside and let God do it.

—Albert Einstein

When I started the research for this book, some friends and colleagues were concerned that I might not be able to find enough "good stories" to fill a book about ordinary grace.

"Look at the world," one friend said. "Grace is a rare thing."

I didn't believe it. I had already opened my eyes and was convinced that, in spite of the many negative and destructive things around us, goodness predominates in the world. It has been a year since I began to focus my attention on grace, and I am more convinced of its ordinariness than ever. My office is overflowing with boxes of notes, letters, and tiny articles from local newspapers throughout the country, thousands of leads that I have not had the time or resources to pursue. When people learned about this book project, they offered many enthusiastic ideas and suggestions, recommendations about people I should talk to. How can something be so rare when everyone, it seems, knows someone whom they describe as especially compassionate or virtuous, someone who regularly acts out of those qualities?

I came home from work one night to find an excited message on my answering machine from the son of my business partner. Justin is fourteen, and we've developed a nice friendship, often talking and bragging about our scores on the computer game Rodent's Revenge. He's normally an animated person, but he was so excited on the phone that I had to listen to his lengthy message twice to make sure I had gotten the story right.

It turned out that Justin had earned twenty dollars that day and had gone to Planet Music—a huge store that sells CDs and tapes—to buy an album. As he was ready to check out, he realized that he didn't have his twenty-dollar bill. He was certain he had had it on his way in, because he had looked at it as he was thinking about which CD he wanted to buy. His mother suggested that he ask one of the managers to see if anyone had found it. "I thought she was crazy," he said. "I said, 'Mom, it's a twenty-dollar bill. My name's not on it. No one could ever tell who it really belonged to. There's no way.' "

Nevertheless, Justin took his mother's advice and asked at the information desk. The manager handed him the twenty, pointed to a young man, and told Justin that "the guy over there in the red shirt turned it in."

"My face turned whiter than white," Justin yelled into the phone. "I couldn't believe it. I mean my money didn't have my name on it. Wouldn't you just think that somebody would keep it? You have to interview him for your book. I talked to him and thanked him. I still can't believe it! He's a college student. His name is Ray. It's spelled R-A-Y. You got that, Kathy? It's R-A-Y. He should be in your book."

My friend Justin had been moved to a near-frenzy by this simple expression of honesty. I couldn't help wondering what the world would be like if we all *expected* decency from each other.

I've learned that ordinary grace occurs in multitudes of tiny actions, sometimes as simple as offering a kind word or returning money found on the floor. The scholar and spiritual translator Eknath Easwaran, who grew up in India, relates a metaphor that his grandmother told him about the power of ordinary people. She showed him a tamarind tree—a big tree with very small, thin leaves. On hot days, the people of Kerala fall asleep in the shade of that tree. On other days, they seek its protection from the rain. Each individual leaf is tiny, but they are so plentiful and packed so close together that they block the sun and rain like one huge canopy. "Little Lamp, you don't have to look for big people," his grandmother taught him. "Look for little people like yourself, then band together and work together in harmony."[1]

How do we understand all the people who, like these slender leaves, together create this great and wonderful canopy of humanity? How is it possible to describe what contributes to the expression of grace around the world? How do we learn to express this grace in our own lives, and most important, how do we teach it to our children?

There are no demographic categories to define the individuals who express goodness. It is impossible to identify any age-range, ethnicity, religious practice, racial group, educational level, or economic class that is predictive of kindness and generosity. Even a person's family background doesn't appear to explain it. A good number of people, in spite of having been raised in desperate circumstances in which love and nurturing were absent, behave with compassion toward others. On the other hand, the news is filled with stories about people who grew up appearing, at least on the surface, to have everything—a nice home, caring parents, a decent standard of living—and ended up committing horrible crimes against others.

Even though there's no formal recipe, no simple combination of attitudes that inevitably brings about grace, there are nevertheless patterns that emerge as one looks at how people find their way to doing good. In the course of my interviews, I identified seven characteristics that appear to be common features of individuals who express ordinary grace:

1. They feel, at a deep level, a strong and clear connection with other people.
2. They have an abiding faith in the goodness of other people.
3. They believe that helping others is not a service but, rather, a privilege and a blessing.

4. They are humble.

5. They have a sense of humor, they describe themselves as "happy," and they give the impression of being psychologically healthy people.

6. Their impulses to do good are immediate and instinctual.

7. They are able to turn negatives, even excruciating suffering, into positive energy and grace.

Feeling the Connections

Most people have little trouble understanding why a person would act generously toward a member of her family, or even toward a close friend. It's easier to understand why a mother or father would donate a kidney to save his or her own child's life than it is to fathom the actions of people like Sal Petras or Mary Groves, each of whom donated a kidney to a casual friend. It is a generally accepted idea, and logical, that compassion is likely to decrease as we experience increasing social distance from someone else. Indeed, social theorists have long claimed that generosity "thins out" as we move further away from our immediate family, kinship group, or clan. When resources are abundant we may be more likely to enlarge our circle of compassion, but when they are limited, it's "family first."

The people I interviewed intuitively recognize their commonality with others and see all of life as intimately related and, most crucial, felt those connections with people outside their own family or social circle. They are informed by the central archetype of wholeness and transpersonal power, which Carl Jung described as "the prompting of the Self," rather than the narrow-minded beliefs of the ego. In a sense these people have "gotten out of their own way." The Bhagavad Gita instructs that "they live in wisdom who see themselves in all and all in them." Buddhist scriptures speak of this oneness, or pure compassion, as the "quivering of the pure heart." And as the Christian philosopher Pierre Teilhard de Chardin wrote, "To overcome every obstacle, to *unite our beings* without loss of individual personality, there is a single force which nothing can replace and nothing can destroy, a force which urges us forwards and draws us upwards: this is the force of love."[2]

Albert Einstein once described the "widening circle of compassion" that an individual experiences as he withdraws from the illusion of detachment: "A human being is part of the whole, called by us 'Universe,' a part limited in time and space. He experiences himself, his thoughts and feelings, as something separated from the rest, a kind of optical delusion of his consciousness. This delusion is a kind of prison for us, restricting us to our personal desires and to affection for a few persons nearest to us. Our task must be to free ourselves from this prison by widening our circle of compassion to embrace all living creatures and the whole of nature in its beauty."[3]

My little brother Jimmy, who is called J.P. these days, and my sister-in-law Deborah are ordinary people. J.P. is the president of a home-building company in the D.C. area, and Deborah is a marketing and promotions consultant and an artist. They live in a dazzling townhouse in an upper-class neighborhood and love to walk to dinners, poetry readings, and movies. On the surface, they appear like most of their baby-boomer contemporaries— fortyish, professional, and well-off. But underneath it all, they are like other people who express ordinary grace: Their contributions are simple and quiet, and their sense of oneness with others is deeply felt.

On Saturdays, J.P. and Deborah deliver meals through an AIDS organization called Food and Friends. This group has delivered more than a million meals to the homebound, the sick, and the dying, and depends on the help of thousands of individual volunteers. In 1996, J.P. was one of three thousand such volunteers who biked the 250-plus miles from Philadelphia to D.C. in an AIDS fund-raiser. Deborah worked on the support team that went ahead of the riders to set up tents and prepare meals.

In 1996, J.P. and Deborah decided to use time off from work to volunteer for Habitat for Humanity. This nonprofit organization's volunteers work directly with the people who will live in the modest homes they construct. The new homeowner is out there with the others, pouring concrete and swinging a hammer. Habitat for Humanity, working in almost every local community, gives families hope for the future by building one house at a time. So far, the group has helped more than 250,000 people in fifty countries move into decent houses. When J.P. and Deborah returned from ten days of helping build homes in Pikeville, Kentucky, I asked them why they chose to spend what most would think of as their "vacation" time pounding nails in ninety-five-degree weather.

"We have so much," J.P. says. "We've got good health and a great family. We have a beautiful house that's cool in the summer and warm in the winter. We eat good food every day. We've got a lot of stuff that you can really live without, too, like a garage-door opener and remote controls for the TV. But our home is just one little sliver of the world, there are so many people who have so little. I have to give something back. I want to instill in the kids the importance of reaching out and helping and also appreciating all the blessings that we all have in our lives."

Deborah echoes these sentiments: "I just look around at how lucky we are. My family taught me that all human beings are important and that we should share what we have. I learned that from the time I was a small child. When you feel the connection with other people, you understand that we are all together in this. The other day I was driving and my air-conditioning wasn't working and it was a hundred degrees. I felt like I was in a little moving oven, and was getting queasy. I had to wait at a light, and on the median, I saw a woman with a cardboard sign—it said 'Homeless, Please Help.' I gave her some money, and at that moment the heat of my car, my sick stomach didn't matter. I was on my way to my air-conditioned luxury townhouse with a fountain and a marble foyer. I'm very lucky."

"We have an inherent stewardship," J.P. says. "That is how

human beings are and can be unless you get too full of yourself, too attached to material trappings. Those things get in the way of feeling the ways in which we are all connected."

Bloodlines don't impress J.P. much, he says. "We're a family of man. There is a spiritual connection between all of us that is right there if you look. That's what I was taught by my parents. Your family is where your heart is. I've been fortunate. Sometimes I think of us as like a pack of wolves. I've got four strong legs and I know where the food is. But there are some gimpy wolves in our pack—they weren't born as lucky as some of the rest of us. I'm strong, I can work with my hands, I should do what I can."

J.P. has very strong, close relationships with both his twenty-two-year-old son, Matthew, and his fifteen-year-old daughter, Katelyn. His sense of connection with others is heightened by his appreciation for the universal concerns of parents. "I watched Kayla, a little girl, on her birthday; she's in a wheelchair. Her parents saved until they could buy some Mylar balloons to tie on her chair. In my job, I'm selling eight-hundred-thousand-dollar houses, working with families who have plenty of money to give their kids a wonderful birthday. But you know what? Kayla's parents feel exactly the same way about her birthday as those wealthy parents do. While we were in Kentucky, we built a home for Benita and her teenage son, Chris. Our worlds seem so different, but we both want exactly the same things. We want to provide a good life for our children, keep them safe, give them everything we can. When you spend time with people who at first appear different, you understand that the truth is that we're exactly the same."

During their time in Kentucky, J.P. and Deborah worked with former President Jimmy Carter and his wife Rosalynn, hundreds of volunteers, and Barry, the brother of Benita, a woman who will move into one of the houses constructed during this week. "Barry is a blessing," says Deborah. He has worked very hard on his sister's house, and drives each day to the site in a 1979 Olds with 300,000 miles on it. When Benita and her son move into their new house, Barry will move into their old trailer. For him, it's a step up in the world, and he's extremely happy about it. Still, he is most excited about going to South Carolina to help build houses for some "really poor people," he says.

"When you see Jimmy Carter with his little baseball cap and red bandanna, and Barry, and Michael and Gabriela from Munich, and hundreds of other people working side by side to give one family a better place to live, you can't miss the connections between all people," says J.P.

"It's like a thunderstorm," says Deborah, "quick and intense. The chances are that you'll never see most of these people again. But you have this immediate sense of relationship with them."

J.P. and Deborah, along with thousands of other volunteers, are living what the ancients knew as the unbroken circle of life, the ways in which we are all part of the whole. This amazing circle spreads itself through all of us, healing the divisions and wounds, illuminating our way, giving meaning to life, and offering the tenderness of grace. A poem written by my brother describes it by its nameless sound:

The rock vibrates, the air is riven
Like ripe fruit splayed on a summer's day
The bird's song is used to call a mate, warn of danger,
Find a nest . . .
If you listen you will hear our universal music
On the street, in the concert hall . . . in the air
It is not the splitting of reeds, the thrumming of strings,
the thrusting of air, or the tambour of skins
It is the passion and yearning to fully become that which we already are . . .
To reach out and express
To become connected and more Whole
Erase the din of noise and hear the music
It is all around.[4]

Believing in the Goodness of Others

There's an old Middle Eastern saying—"Trust Allah, but tie your camel to a post"—which attests to the paradoxical need to believe in the benevolence of a higher power while at the same time recognizing the existence of thievery and other evil. It would be foolish, even reckless, to believe that wickedness is not a part of our world. Indeed, to deny the existence of the shadow, the dark aspects of human nature, is to create a psychological state in which evil is most likely to be enacted. People who display ordinary grace live in the same world and encounter the same problems as you and I do; they are fully aware that life can be dangerous, that not everyone can be trusted, and that it is sometimes necessary to protect oneself.

And yet, in spite of their awareness of the realities of our world, the people I interviewed seemed to understand intuitively that "no human beings are as good as their public best, nor as bad as their private worst." Never allowing themselves to assume the worst of people, their anticipation was always for goodness. They didn't judge reflexively, and seemed willing to believe in the decency of another person, and to reach out and make connections with people on that basis.

When one looks for the good in others, compassion ceases to be an abstract concept and, instead, reverberates in the concrete moment of a personal connection—in the "minute particulars" of the relationship, as William Blake called them. Living this way allows one to find a "precious moment of true intimacy," as the founder of the Catholic Worker movement, Dorothy Day, put it. "I have some grand notions in my head," she said, "but they often fall by the wayside when I'm sitting at the table talking with one person, hearing all that has happened in that one life."[5] Heartfelt compassion engenders a similar kindness in others, and as when a stone is thrown into a lake, the ripples radiate out and touch every shore.

A good friend of mine named Teresa Roberts has been working with people with HIV and AIDS since the very early stages of the epidemic. Recently she organized workshops at Camp Wakonda, a wonderful program staffed by volunteers that helps families with children who are HIV-positive or have AIDS. The camp offers time out from doctor's visits, blood tests, and the stares and cruelties that most of these children are accustomed to. During four summer days, these kids are given the freedom to be just kids—canoeing, hiking, playing games, and learning crafts. The adult caregivers (usually the children's parents, grandparents, or foster parents) participate in workshops that focus on everything from healthy nutrition to foot massage. Getting to know these families convinced Teresa Roberts that grace is not just about doing good, but also about recognizing the inherent goodness in every human being and the reciprocal relationships that evolve when people feel a connection to one another. "You can go around doing good for days," she tells me, "but it doesn't matter unless people are open to their own goodness and their own ability to trust, to receive." Teresa believes that this kind of openness—this sense of goodness existing in everyone—allows for a true feeling of "hospitality." She reminds me that the word *hospitality* means to welcome the stranger in. Along with this welcoming comes a vulnerability, the need to show real trust in the basic goodness of the person being welcomed. "It isn't about trying to get it all right—like in a Martha Stewart world. It's an understanding that I trust in your goodness. Whatever is going to happen to me in your presence is okay," Teresa says.

Organizations across the country are embracing this kind of hospitality—welcoming the stranger—through people who emphasize the goodness in all of us as a starting point for community. A variety of alternative cafés have sprung up with this idea in mind and make it their mission to provide more than just food to homeless people in their neighborhoods. Seen as an alternative to more traditional services for the homeless and hungry, these cafés offer nutritious meals in gracious and safe settings, with table service, fresh flowers, art-covered walls, and jazz playing in the background. "Meals are a service, but on their own they're not what change people's homelessness and poverty and hunger," says Genny Nelson, co-founder (with Sandy Gooch) and executive director of the oldest of the alternative cafés, Sisters of the Road, in Portland, Oregon. "Sandy and I listened carefully to the stories of men and women who ate in the soup lines as their only means of meeting nutritional needs, and we went and tried those lines ourselves. I can tell you it is a humbling experience," she says.

Sandy and Genny knew what they wanted to create for their neighborhood. They started with three goals: to make a safe place for everyone, and especially for women and children; to offer nourishing meals and make them affordable to all people; to offer job training and work experience.

"We talked to a lot of people, but I was very struck by something that one of our future customers said: 'Create a place where I can barter my labor instead of my soul.' "

At Sisters of the Road Café—the name is the hobo slang for women who hitch rides on freight cars—a meal costs a dollar twenty-five, or a dollar in food stamps. Those without money can work in exchange for food. At a rate of five dollars an hour, the typical guest can earn enough for a meal in fifteen minutes of washing windows, recycling, or clearing tables. The Sisters don't believe in doing things for people that they can do for themselves.

Genny Nelson tells me a story about a woman from the neighborhood who barged into a staff meeting at a local social service agency. The woman, Genny says, was "mad as a hatter." She started sobbing and said, "I'm new here. I'm from a rural area and don't know where to go for help. But don't ever forget that I have gifts to offer too—I have things to bring to the table."

"We opened Sisters of the Road Café with that woman's words in our hearts," Genny says. "She said something that was so true—about everyone bringing gifts. The gifts go back and forth among us and we'll solve these problems together. We all need to be around the table to share the resources and the goodness that everyone brings."

Genny tells me another story about a homeless woman who lived under a bridge and who was in the café one day as several people were talking about a baby girl and the things she needed. The next day, the homeless woman walked into the café carrying a pair of booties for the baby. "She had nothing, but she found some way to get those booties," Genny says. "I would never romanticize poverty—it is a harsh and dreadful way of life—but even here there is joy in very small things; there is sharing even when there is almost nothing to share."

These and other stories—the thousands of people who pooled their resources to build the Barzachs' playground—show us how we may move toward a future filled with mutual respect and fellowship, a truly multicultural, multiracial human family, working together to solve our common problems. Families that benefit from Habitat for Humanity often become the most active volunteers, and pass along the blessing by building a house for someone else. People donate organs, a life is saved, and those who are given this new life find their own ways of serving and helping others. A woman with nothing finds something to give to a baby she has never met. This poem by the seventeenth-century Japanese poet Bashō describes with elegant simplicity the way such goodness moves and reverberates:

The temple bell stops
but the sound keeps coming
out of the flowers.

Service Is a Blessing for the One Who Serves

In the film *Marvin's Room*, there is a moving scene between two sisters who have been estranged for fifteen years. The older one, Bessie, played by Diane Keaton, has stayed at home to care for their ailing father and their eccentric aunt, and is now dying of leukemia. Her younger sister, Lee, played by Meryl Streep, left years earlier to pursue her own life and has come home to Florida to determine if she or either of her two sons can donate bone marrow for a transplant—her big sister's only hope for survival. When the doctor calls, they learn that no one in the family can be a bone-marrow donor for Bessie.

"It's been a good life for me. I've been very lucky to have had so much love," Bessie tells her sister through her tears.

"I know," Lee says. "They've loved you very much."

"Well, yes, but, I mean, I've been the lucky one, to have been able to love so much," Bessie answers.

When the heart is open, it is a blessing to give one's compassion to others. When we see a sick child or a hungry person, true compassion demands that we suffer along with that person, and lessening the sufferer's pain also relieves our own. What might have started as something done for another ends up nurturing the self: Every act of love benefits the giver as much as the receiver.

Without exception, all of the people I spoke with focused on *how good it feels to them* to know that they can do something to help another person. They told me that compassionate actions gave them a greater sense of meaning and fulfillment in their own lives. Not a single person cited sentimentality or pity as motivation for their actions. Instead, they understood important things about our common human condition. "There, but for the grace of God, go I," many said.

And many experienced a vibrant spirituality and felt close not only to other people but also to God, as they were helping others. Wayne Muller, a minister and therapist who works closely with the poor and homeless, with cancer and AIDS patients, and with teenage delinquents, describes his feelings about opening his heart: "Whenever I become aware of another's suffering, I invariably feel myself in the presence of something both sacred and deeply human, something fundamental and true that offers a glimpse into the nature of all things."[6] Even those who do not consider themselves "religious" or "spiritual" reported experiencing a powerful awakening to feelings of universality and justice.

A Hasidic parable tells of the divine power of mutual support and caring: A man is taken by a guide to see a vision of the afterlife. First he is taken to a great hall with a long banquet table filled with delicious food. There are many people sitting at the table, and each has a three-foot-long spoon. No matter how they contort their bodies, their spoons are too long to put even a single bite into their mouths. They sit alongside each other, hungry and in mutual misery.

"This is Hell," says the guide.

The man is then taken to another place—an identical hall, with an identical banquet table set with the same magnificent food and unwieldy three-foot-long spoons. But here everyone is joyous, healthy, and well-fed.

"This is Heaven," the guide says.

The man is confused. "I don't understand the difference," he says.

"In Heaven," the guide tells him, as he points to someone lifting his long-handled spoon to the waiting lips of a neighbor, "they have learned to feed each other."[7]

Ordinary Grace Is Humble

Franz Kafka observed that "humility provides everyone, even him who despairs in solitude, with the strongest relationship to his fellow man." Humility is a natural precursor to the expression of ordinary grace; it's hard to be elbow-deep in chicken soup to feed the poor, or pounding nails to build a house for a homeless family, or sitting in a dimly lit hospital room in the middle of the night and holding the hand of a young man dying with AIDS, and still have an inflated ego.

Like the word "humility," derived from *humus,* which refers to the organic portion of soil, people who reflect grace are grounded in everyday things and get their hands dirty working with the stuff of life. The love and grace they embody erase the duality between spirit and matter, bringing soul down to earth. Henry David Thoreau was right when he wrote, "Humility like darkness reveals the heavenly lights."[8]

Tom and Mickey Giles understand what it means to come from humble beginnings. Tom was born in an insane asylum to a sixteen-year-old mother who had already given birth to three other children; he was beaten regularly by his father and forced to work in a sawmill. When he was eight, he became a ward of the state and was placed in foster care. The foster home where he lived was looked upon as a moneymaking venture by the family who organized it, so he never really felt loved by anyone. At eighteen he left home and joined the Marine Corps, and then spent three tours of duty in Vietnam. He has all the demographic characteristics— born to a teenage mother, abused as a child, raised without love— that characterize people who struggle to make something of themselves. But instead of being an embittered person, he's a kindly bear of a man with an easy laugh and an obvious humility, someone known by local kids as the "Motorcycle Santa."

I met Tom and his wife Mickey on a beautiful Sunday afternoon at Sunrise Auto and Motorcycle Shop, where they are working on a "Quiz Run" race to raise money for a local charity. It's a clear Virginia spring day, and the parking lot is filled with brightly colored motorcycles of all sizes and shapes. The smell of oil is in the air, and the noise of the engines is deafening. The riders have been given a specific route and will find the answers to questions posed by a crossword puzzle if they complete the course correctly. Each rider pays a six-dollar entry fee, and after a small prize is given to the winner, the rest of the money will be donated to a charity that gathers toys, clothes, and other supplies for people living in poverty.

Tom and Mickey are out here on every Sunday afternoon when it doesn't rain, and they're always doing the same thing—raising money for people in need. With a group of other bikers, they have "adopted" a decaying and battered trailer park which Tom says looks as if it's been hit by a tornado. They have sponsored holiday meals and gifts for needy families, delivered presents to hospitalized children, raised funds for multiple sclerosis, and contributed to schools for handicapped children. Every November and December, Tom and Mickey make dozens of weekend visits to hospitals and special schools for children. They dress as Santa and Mrs. Claus, and arrive with other bikers dressed up as elves. Mickey straps herself into a sleigh that's filled with presents and covered with candy canes and Christmas lights. The whole assemblage is pulled by Tom's 1983 Yamaha Venture Royale motorcycle. "The reindeer," he tells the children, "are in New York."

What motivates this ordinary couple to give their spare time so freely to others? They both work hard for a living: Tom is a superintendent for a commercial construction company, and Mickey is the district manager for Piece Goods Shops. And, like most of us, on top of their long hours they have the regular chores that go with being homeowners. So why do they go out of their way to help others? "It's our job," Mickey says simply. "I grew up on a farm and even though I had a loving family, we never had anything. I don't want children to grow up as poor as I was. If you can touch one person, if every one of us would do his part, there wouldn't be children who have to go to bed hungry or who never get a present at Christmas."

Tom tells me that he "just plain loves kids." He remembers what his life was like as a child and doesn't want to see other children suffer as he did. "I know that these kids feel just the same ways that I did," he says. He looks out toward the sea of motorcycles getting ready to start the Quiz Run. "It's not like any one of us has anything extra, but we want to make sure to share what we do have," he says. His eyes fill with tears, as they have each time we've talked about the children whose lives are so dramatically affected by poverty and illness. Tom and Mickey understand that compassion is present in the smell of the oil and the roaring motorcycle engines as they squeal out of the parking lot on this spring morning.

The Jungian analyst Marion Woodman celebrates this simple truth: "Real love happens when embodied soul meets embodied soul," she writes. "Not in spirit, not in that disembodied world where we want to be perfect, but in life, when we're changing the diapers of someone we love who is dying of cancer, swabbing their lips; when we're doing things we didn't think we could do, when we're stripped of all pride. Our friend is stripped, we are stripped. There is no false modesty. We are stripped of everything that is unreal, and the two of us are there together. I can't even put it into words. Where soul meets soul, that's love."[9]

An ancient Jewish proverb teaches that we usually fail to see God because we have forgotten how to stoop low enough. Just three months before his death, Carl Jung said, "The voice of God can still be perceived if one is only humble enough." So it is with grace, surrounding us and intimately present at every moment here in our very human world. Seeking spiritual wisdom doesn't require studying with a guru or retreating to an ashram or monastery to pray. Blessings are found not only at the tops of pristine mountains but also in the gutters and back alleys of everyday life. They flourish in soup kitchens, cornfields, grimy inner-city shelters, nursing homes, animal refuges, along the banks of polluted rivers, and even in the extraordinary world of cyberspace. They surround us at the Wal-Mart, the local gas station, the classroom, and on the sidewalk in front of your house, as you go about every uneventful moment of daily life. The most profound depths of spirituality are present, as the Zen tradition says, while we "chop wood and carry water." "If your philosophy doesn't grow corn," said Sun Bear, a Native American shaman, "I don't want to hear about it." The opportunity for love is ever-present, and in every place; its manifestation relies only on free will, on our decision at any given moment to receive a gift from a loving universe.

Among the people I interviewed, I found no preaching, no judgments about what others should be doing, no complex philosophical systems, and no attempts to proselytize to anyone. Not one claimed any special enlightenment—a good rule of thumb is that anyone who claims to be specially enlightened probably isn't. The humility they showed reminded me of a story I had heard about Mahatma Gandhi. A reporter rushing after a train begged Gandhi to give him a message of spiritual wisdom that he could take back to his village. As the train began to move, Gandhi scribbled one sentence on a piece of paper bag and handed it to him. It said simply: "My life is my message."[10]

Humor, Happiness, and Psychological Health

Q: What does the Zen Buddhist say at the hot dog stand?
A: "Make me One with everything."

In 1995, my brother and sister-in-law, J.P. and Deborah, spent their summer vacation along with J.P.'s kids, Matthew and Katelyn, at the Oglala Sioux reservation in Pine Ridge, South Dakota. They'd gone there to work with hundreds of volunteers to repair ramshackle houses, the kind where water pours in through broken roofs, drywall rots away, and the wind blows through holes in the walls. Within a few days on the reservation, they'd each been given a tribal name by the Oglala people. Deborah, covered in drywall mud and a favorite with the local children, was called "Laughs A Lot"—a "sacred" name, she says, because it was given to her by children. After spending several days fixing up the wrong building with his team, J.P. was named "Wrong-Way." "I'll tell you," he says, "everything depends upon how you start out. You head out in the wrong direction on that desert at the very start and you don't know where you'll end up. We did do a very nice job of painting the wrong building, though." For the whole week that J.P. and Deborah were in South Dakota, laughter became the language they shared with these people as they worked together. Having started out as strangers just a day or so earlier, they had quickly become friends. Even as they were leaving, a young Sioux boy at the tiny Pine Ridge airport asked J.P., "Hey, you're Wrong-Way, aren't you? I want to shake your hand!"

In A.D. 33, the Greek philosopher Philo observed that "God is the creator of laughter that is good." The people I interviewed for this book seemed to have an amazing capacity for taking the world's problems seriously while never taking themselves too seriously. They seemed to experience genuine joy and pleasure at the opportunities and challenges before them, and I noticed that they laughed often and had a good time. Their sense of humor was creative, spontaneous, philosophical, and even slightly self-deprecating, but never hostile or condescending toward others. It expressed itself instead in an easygoing attitude that seemed to naturally embrace the humorous edge of things.

Standing in a hot and dusty community vegetable patch in an

impoverished town on Virginia's Eastern Shore with a group of volunteers for Hope's Garden, I'm being shown how much things have grown this year. For more than an hour, we've been talking in the hot sun about plans for fruit trees and flower beds, and I'm amazed at how much we are laughing, what a good time we're having. One woman tells me, "If people only knew what a great time we have out here, we'd be swamped with volunteers!" All of these people on the Eastern Shore would describe themselves as living full lives and meeting every day with life-validating enthusiasm. Not one of them seems to feel burdened by the decision to act with generosity. I hear no complaints about all of the hours that their service to others is taking away from their responsibilities or their leisure time, nor any expression of regret about the decisions and choices that they have made. Instead, they feel pure pleasure in what they are doing.

This is not to say that none of them has any problems or suffers bad moods—they're not saints on earth. Healthy, normal human beings all experience sadness, hurt, guilt, anger, grief, anxiety, and frustration from time to time. But in studying mature, "self-actualized" people, the psychologist Abraham Maslow described precisely what I've seen: he wrote that "psychologically healthy people are more able to enjoy, to love, to laugh, to have fun, to be humorous, to be silly, to be whimsical and fantastic, to be pleasantly 'crazy,' and to permit and value and enjoy emotional experiences in general and peak experiences in particular and to have them more often."[11]

I couldn't help contrasting these people with those I've encountered in my work as a clinical psychologist. As a therapist, I see clients every day whose lives are burdened with sadness, loneliness, and a deep sense of alienation. Psychologists are trained to issue a diagnosis, to find a specific disease at work, but this is usually inappropriate. The majority of the people I have worked with do not have illnesses—they have simply lost sight of why they are here. Experiencing a spiritual rather than a medical problem, they have never learned (or cannot remember) what it means to give and receive love unconditionally. They have forgotten that, even in the midst of great suffering, their spirit remains steadfast and true.

I reflected on what it is about feeling a connection with others and helping them that leads to greater happiness in life, and I can't stop thinking about the people whose stories I've told: they seem to be happier, to have a greater sense of meaning in their lives, to be more grounded than usual, and to cherish laughter and good times. Were they psychologically healthier to begin with, or has helping others caused them to heal their wounds and become fully alive? What if the simple act of expressing love and compassion, and doing so with a sense of humor, actually changes a person?

In the thirteenth century, St. Bonaventure wrote: "Since happiness is nothing else but the enjoyment of the Supreme good, and the Supreme good is above us, no one can be happy who does not rise above himself."

Impulses to Do Good
Are Immediate and Instinctual

In 1989, playwright Teddy Gross was walking down an urban street with his three-year-old daughter, Nora. The little girl asked him if they could take home the cold and hungry man who had just asked them for money. "I wanted to encourage her concern," he says. "But I was at a loss for a realistic way to take action." As soon as they got home, Teddy and Nora began to put their pennies together and were soon asking their neighbors to do the same. Teddy took the idea of "harvesting pennies" to his synagogue and, almost immediately, they raised more than $25,000. Nora's and Teddy's instinctive desire to help became the simple beginning of Common Cents—a national school-based program in which children have raised more than $750,000 in pennies to help supply soup kitchens, buy clothes for homeless people, make donations to disaster relief programs, and support reading programs for kids.[12]

Nineteen-year-old Keshia Thomas did not intend to become a hero when she joined three hundred others protesting a Ku Klux Klan rally in Ann Arbor, Michigan. When the crowd converged on a white man wearing Confederate flags on his vest and T-shirt, Keshia, a young black woman, wanted to ask him, "What did I ever do to you?" But the crowd quickly got out of control and began kicking and beating him. Appalled, Keshia threw herself over the fallen man and shielded him from the crowd and their onslaught. A photograph, taken at the rally, of this teenage girl protecting a man who only moments earlier had been the target of her protest, is a stunning symbol of the suddenness with which a powerful empathy can manifest itself. "He's still somebody's child," she said simply, when asked why she had done what she did.[13]

The people I interviewed don't sit home and mull over what they should or shouldn't be doing for others. They don't waffle. When they see a need, they simply respond to it. For all of them, acting with compassion has become a habit. "Isn't helping other people just how you're supposed to live?" one eighty-five-year-old woman asked me. "If some good can come out of tragedy and help someone else then I'll know I made the right decision," said a mother who donated her son's organs to unknown recipients. "People need to eat every day, so why shouldn't I deliver food every day?" remarked a woman who has made it her personal mission to bring her impoverished neighbors at least one good meal a day. "You can't see suffering and not want to do something to relieve it," said a man who takes time from his medical practice to feed the homeless. In the same way that a hero rushes into a burning building or dives into the water to save a drowning person, the people I interviewed act with no thought, no deliberations, just clear and present action.

Turning Negatives into Positives

Like many who experience a devastating loss, Peter and Amy Barzach were searching for a way to make sense of the death of their infant son. Instead of burrowing into their grief, they decided to pull themselves through their pain and were inspired even to create a lasting tribute to his brief life. From their deep sorrow they created a playground where *all* children could play together. Volunteers for Habitat for Humanity see people living in squalor and poverty and use their hammers to build new homes and new lives for them. Susan and Bill Belfiore walked into a shadow world of despair and hopelessness when they entered that Romanian orphanage, and they emerged with a vibrant and beautiful family. Charles Horton, Richard Andrews, and Jack Powell—all physicians operating in difficult, distressing situations—have each found ways of bringing light into dark places.

As I began to research and write this book, I was given a gift of extraordinary grace myself, something which emerged from a situation touched by sorrow. I am very blessed to have both editors and a literary agent who understand my thinking about ordinary grace. My agent, Lisa Ross, who over the years has become a very good friend, happened to mention this book to her brother Steve. He was invariably polite about, but not always interested in, the books that Lisa represented; yet quite to her surprise, he was very taken by the idea of a book about ordinary people doing exceptionally good things. He, too, believed that goodness is far more common than most people might think. In fact, Lisa felt that Steve might be a good person to interview for this book.

Steve understood ordinary grace so well because he lived it

every day. He was the kind of person who was always interested in the well-being of people he met as he went about his life, and thus he quite easily made friends out of strangers. A teacher and an artist, Steve began working with the Teacher Corps, a domestic program associated with the Peace Corps, in the early 1970s. He became an active participant in strengthening the United Nations' mission to forge international friendships and create peace. "I believe in doing, not just thinking. I'm committed to action," Steve told a reporter during an interview in 1995.

During the course of his life, Steve developed programs for young students that allowed them to combine their academic skills with community service. He created a mentoring program in a California middle school in which students would tutor younger children, assist the blind, serve food at a soup kitchen, or lend a hand to elderly people. These students would then write about and discuss their experiences. The principal of the school in which Steve taught was overwhelmed after reading their essays. "You can tell they really got something that will last a lifetime out of that experience," he said.

Tragically, Steve's work would be cut short. At age forty-seven, he was dying of AIDS. But, even as his health was failing, he continued to make certain that his community-service program continued. "He was always focused outward," Lisa tells me. "Everyone has his own little circle, but Steve's was enormous and included a great diversity of people."

During the first week of October 1996, as I was starting to write this book, I received a package from Steve. It contained a short note and a bit of calligraphy that he had done, represent-ing the word "grace." "I thought you might appreciate this," he wrote. "At just the time I began to be drawn toward Sumi callig-raphy for the concise beauty of its symbolic communication, my sister Lisa, with typical synchronicity, sent me a book with all the perfectly appropriate characters, of which 'grace' is my favorite."

The calligraphy that Steve sent me is an ancient pictogram of a person resting on a square mat, above the symbol for "heart." It means that *the one who rests upon the heart achieves grace.*

Steve died on October 27, 1996, and I found myself grieving for a man I had never met—a man, aware that he was in the final days of his life, who found it somehow important to send his remarkable gift to a stranger. Steve's drawing is framed and hang-ing on the wall over my computer. Throughout the course of writing this book, I have looked at it often and hoped that I would remain true to and always grateful for its blessing—that I would honor the grace I felt flowing from Steve and the others I'd interviewed. This drawing has helped me to understand in new ways the importance of awakening the heart, of never being afraid of its pain, and of always operating from its longing to express love and compassion. Chögyam Trungpa comments elo-quently about this tenderness of the heart; how it is impossible to describe its depths when we soften and open ourselves to our true natures. "When you awaken your heart, you find to your surprise that your heart is empty," he writes. "If you search for the awakened heart, if you put your hand through your rib cage and feel for it, there is nothing there but tenderness. You feel sore and soft, and if you open your eyes to the rest of the world, you feel tremendous sadness. . . . It occurs because your heart is completely open, exposed. It is the pure raw heart. . . . It is this tender heart of a warrior that has the power to heal the world."[14]

10.

Finding Grace
in Your Own Life

The winds of grace are always blowing,

but you have to raise the sail.

—Ramakrishna

Jean-François Gravelet, called Blondin, was a famous tight-rope walker and acrobat who lived during the nineteenth century. His most notable feat was to cross Niagara Falls on a tightrope without a safety net. To keep the audiences growing and the regulars coming back for more, he would increase the level of difficulty each time he performed the stunt. During his career, Blondin crossed the Falls in several daring ways: blind-folded, on stilts, even in a sack. One of his most dangerous feats was to push a wheelbarrow loaded with a sack of cement while gingerly balancing on the tightrope. The cement was so heavy that the slightest wrong move in any direction could fling him to certain death. He performed the feat many times. "Do you believe I can do anything on a high wire?" he asked a reporter covering the story. "Oh yes, Mr. Blondin," said the reporter, "after what I've witnessed today, I believe you can do anything."

"Do you believe that instead of a sack of cement, I could put a man in this wheelbarrow—a man who has never been on a tightrope before—and wheel him safely to the other side without a safety net?"

"Oh, yes, Sir, Mr. Blondin. I believe it," said the reporter.

"Good," said Blondin. "Get in."

We might genuinely trust the skills of this high-wire expert— seeing is believing—but how many of us would willingly get into that wheelbarrow? Thinking about our spiritual beliefs or observing them in the actions of others is far easier for most people than actually living them. But this is precisely what every religion and wisdom tradition teaches us—to "get in," and *live* the truth of our beliefs. It is not enough to simply worship at a church, synagogue, or mosque, or to practice meditation or yoga. It is, as an old Spanish proverb teaches, "not the same to talk of bulls as it is to be in the bullring."

To express ordinary grace it is necessary to manifest our faith. Whether that faith arises from traditional religious beliefs, a strong sense of social justice, or a deeply held feeling of kinship and unity with other living beings and the earth itself, it means nothing until it is put to use. Former president Jimmy Carter's mission for social action, as expressed by Habitat for Humanity and by the Carter Foundation in Atlanta, is a wonderful example of Christian beliefs in action. In his book *Living Faith*, he talks of his commitment to putting his spiritual conviction to use: "Throughout these three-score and ten years, my faith as a Christian has provided the necessary stability in my life. Come to think of it, stability is not exactly the right word, because to have faith in something is an inducement not to dormancy but to action."[1]

In 1979, an ex–aerospace engineer and full-time Zen Buddhist priest named Bernard Glassman established the Greystone Foundation in Yonkers, New York, which at the time had the highest per-capita rate of homelessness in the nation. Using entrepreneurial strategies, Glassman and volunteers have transformed their community: today, formerly homeless people are earning a living wage, participating in community life, and teaching others marketable skills. All of the activities at Greystone are based on the Buddhist philosophy of "loving-kindness," and on the importance of integrating economic, social, educational, and spiritual dimensions into all of one's work. In his lovely book *Instructions to the Cook*—the title comes from the Zen metaphor that living life fully constitutes the "supreme meal"—Glassman makes it clear that one's own life is both the greatest gift one can receive and the most important offering one can make. "The course of social action grows naturally out of the courses of spirituality and livelihood," he writes. "Recognizing the oneness of life, we naturally reach out to other people because we realize that we are not separate from them."[2]

Bernard Glassman's Zen point of view is shared by other prominent Buddhists. The Dalai Lama, for example, has repeatedly emphasized that compassion should not be seen as a lofty ideal but must be made part of our everyday behavior. "Action is much more important than simply praying," he says. "Unless our insights result in some practical action, they are not useful at all. . . . With compassion, one needs to be engaged, involved."[3]

Eighty-year-old Sister Mary Joan Kentz agrees. She had always thought that when she reached retirement age, she would slow down and teach at a convent for her order, the Sisters of Notre Dame de Namur. But it was this diminutive nun who brought the first—and only—program for children with HIV and AIDS to the sprawling Tidewater, Virginia, area. Once she recognized the appalling lack of support and medical services for these kids, she sprang into action and created the Children's AIDS Network Designed for Interfaith Involvement, known as CANDII House. Sister Mary Joan insists that there were many, many people who made this program a reality, but the people who were there say that it was this little nun who made it all happen. "We think we're in charge but this is really God's plan," she tells me. "In God's good time something will happen that will be more astounding than anything I could ever even dream about. That doesn't mean you sit still and wait for something to drop out of the sky. You turn over every stone."

One of America's favorite Christian hymns, "Amazing Grace," was written in the eighteenth century by John Newton, a

British sea captain. While many people are touched by the words and enjoy singing it, most don't realize that its author was the captain of a slave ship. Transporting more than six hundred people at a time, he sailed from Africa to America and the West Indies. He made this voyage for many years until, during a violent storm, he experienced an epiphany and realized he was contributing to the evil in the world. He turned his ship around in mid-ocean, returned the slaves to their own land, and sailed home to England. For the last forty-three years of his life he studied the Bible, became a minister, and preached the gospel in London and Olney.

Like John Newton and his sudden burst of conscience, our society is changing. More and more people are questioning the values they live by. Most of us are not as evil as John Newton was in supporting a vile practice like slavery, of course, and are therefore not as likely to experience an epiphany. But many of us are isolated, lonely, self-absorbed, and overwhelmed by the demands of daily life. We seek meaning but don't know how to find it. We want to be happy and excited about being alive, but we discover all of our habitual strategies come up cold. Perhaps we've grown weary of living without the experience of grace. But, individually and collectively, we seem to be undergoing a paradigm shift—a fundamental change in the ways that we see the world. With increasing frequency, people are asking, "Who am I?" and "What is my purpose in life?"

Like John Newton, we want to turn the ship around. While it would be impossible to answer that question for everyone, there are nevertheless some universal strategies that can help. These are my suggestions:

1. *Wake up.* The first step to making any kind of change in your life requires that you awaken. But coming to a new, higher level of consciousness doesn't happen overnight. Instead, you're more likely to go through a process of integrating fresh insights that will culminate in newfound wisdom. There are many different approaches to individuation and consciousness, and everyone must seek his or her own path, but questions such as "Who am I?" and "What is my purpose in life?" are a good way to start the journey. My earlier book, *Awakening at Midlife*,[4] described a number of strategies for delving into these questions, as do the many other books that focus on our need for spiritual nourishment. In fact, every great religion and wisdom tradition speaks to these central human concerns. Read, study, and explore them. As the revered Indian poet Kabir wrote, "Wake up, wake up! You have slept millions and millions of years. Why not wake up this morning?"

Remember that each of us has the power to determine what he or she chooses to tune in to. We can simply make a decision to look at the world differently, to awaken to the goodness that surrounds us in every moment. It is not fate but a choice, as to whether we will carry the burden of bitterness, fear, and distrust, or open our hearts to the great cosmic dance of life. The possibility of finding grace is endless and everywhere—in our families, in our peers, in the strangers on the street, and in ourselves. Awakening—following the path that calls us by the heart—is the first essential step. Rumi understands that the possibility for such an awakening is ever-present and can happen in an instant. "God is right here," he writes, "closer than your own breath."

2. *Discover what you love.* Ask yourself: "What is important in my life? What is missing from it?" Very often, these questions will reveal what you need to do differently in order to live fully and authentically. If the questions become lost in your whirling thoughts, take twenty minutes each day to meditate, to let your mind be free and allow the images and thoughts there to present themselves. Ask yourself, "What is in my heart?" You already know the answers. The Ibo people of Nigeria have a proverb: "It is the heart that gives, the fingers just let go." Look to your heart and you will find that your life will overflow with meaning and passion. A Yaqui sorcerer named Don Juan explained the power of this way of life beautifully to Carlos Castaneda when he said: "For me there is only the traveling on paths that have heart, on any path that may have heart. There I travel, and the only worthwhile challenge is to traverse its full length. And there I travel, looking, looking, breathlessly."[5]

3. *Be prepared for pain as well as joy.* Compassion shows itself in thousands of acts every day. It is the same with suffering. When we see all the pain in the world there can be a natural tendency to want to look the other way. And so we should be warned: It

hurts to care, to open the heart to the pain of others. And yet, the removal of barriers between ourselves and others has a mysterious nurturing force as well. The idea of spiritual seeking as an exclusively inward endeavor, seeking the "emptiness" or quietness of meditation, cloistering our own emotions as a way of transcending the world, is not the path that all the great religions and wisdom traditions present to us. Instead, we are urged to move toward the world, to participate *in* the suffering, to transform it, and to create a metanoia—a "change of heart."

This is the meaning behind the Hebrew story in which we are instructed always to assume that the person sitting next to you is the Messiah waiting for some simple human kindness. It is what Mother Teresa meant when she described her work with the sick and dying people of Calcutta as "caring for my beloved Christ in his most distressing disguises." It is what the Dalai Lama expresses when he says, "My religion is simple—my religion is kindness." The Hindu salutation *namaste* sums it all up—it means "the god in me recognizes the god in you." Remember that ordinary grace requires opening ourselves up as much to the suffering of others as to their happiness. In this humble act, we recognize our unity. We find joy inside our sorrow.

4. *Start where you are.* Expressing grace doesn't require anything more than your commitment to do so. Take a deep breath and decide that you want to be kinder, more generous, and more compassionate, and it will happen. You don't have to journey beyond your own neighborhood, your own family, your own life,

to express grace. A good friend of mine named Alice Broome is one of thousands of volunteers who help to clean up Chesapeake Bay each year. "This is *our* neighborhood," she says. "If everyone would do just a little bit, we would restore the beauty and the health of this magnificent natural resource for everyone who comes here and for ourselves as well." Every neighborhood and community—including our own—offers opportunities to put grace into action.

Sometimes starting where you are is not as much about geography as it is about personal experience, about opening up and "going public" with one's own painful experiences as a way of helping others to make the same journey. Actor Robert Urich struggled with and overcame synovial sarcoma, an extremely rare and typically fatal form of soft-tissue cancer. He realized just how important emotional support and a positive attitude were in his own struggle with this disease, and he wanted to share his insights with others. Today this popular actor devotes a great deal of his time to speaking to cancer-support groups throughout the country, bringing his message of hope and healing to other people who are battling cancer. Songwriter and musician Beth Nielsen Chapman tragically lost her fifty-year-old husband, Ernest, to a rare form of lymphoma in August 1994. She transformed her sorrow into remarkable, healing music, and now invites audience members and others to join her after her concerts for mutual support, music, and conversation about reconstructing sorrow into creative and compassionate energy through workshops that she calls Art and Loss.

An American Buddhist nun named Pema Chödrön, in her wonderful book *Start Where You Are,* underscores the ways that anyone can express compassion in his or her own life.[6] Chödrön says that we already have everything we need to express ordinary grace surrounding us at every moment. "We are one blink of an eye away from being fully awake," she says.

Look around you. There are so many people and places right in your own community, your own neighborhood, crying out for your spirit and energy. Their happiness awaits you. You only have to start where you are.

5. Simplify and scale down. Our lives have become so filled with irrelevancies that we often allow no time for grace to enter. Look honestly at what is important to you. How often do those meaningful things get shoved into the background of your daily life? What *is* your daily life, anyway? Are you happy? Are you working around the clock in order to maintain a fancy home that you never have the time to enjoy? Is there not a spare moment to contemplate the truth of your own life?

More and more people are questioning their values and lifestyles, and are discovering a desire to simplify matters. Seduced by the consumer culture and the financial rewards of hard work, many of us have a great deal of material wealth, but because of the demands and complexities of modern life, we have not found a lot of happiness to go along with it. Joe Dominguez and Vicki Robin, in their book *Your Money or Your Life,* describe the importance of finding a "new road map," a new way of thinking about our lives and seeing the need for integrating all of our values.[7] Author Elaine St. James discovered that when she and her husband simplified their lives, they freed up more than thirty hours a week that could be spent on other, more important things.[8] Would an extra thirty hours a week give you enough time to volunteer at a soup kitchen, to work with a food bank, to tutor a child, or to watch a sunset with an elderly neighbor who lives alone?

The more one listens simply and clearly to one's heart, the more one's priorities fall into place and the irrelevancies start to seem like just that. The process of simplifying grows naturally out of the search for grace, and they support and amplify each other. The ancient Taoist words of Lao-tzu, written in the sixth century, offer wisdom for our modern age:

Manifest plainness,
Embrace simplicity,
Reduce selfishness,
Have few desires.

6. *Recognize the spiritual ties between people.* Regardless of which religion or philosophy we subscribe to as individuals, if we look carefully, we notice that all the great traditions teach the same truths about how we are to live in the world. "Every religion," writes religious scholar Huston Smith, "is a blend of universal principles and local setting."[9] Grace depends not so much on what is written in holy scriptures but on what is known in the hearts of people

around the world. All religions teach that there is a divine reality beyond the material world, that there exists a spiritual universe transcending our visible, outer reality, and that some form of creative intelligence, called by hundreds of different names—God, Universal Mind, Yahweh, Christ, Jah, Brahman, the Great Spirit, Allah, Tao, That Art Thou—is the ground of all being.

To know these truths is to dwell in this unity, and to dwell in this unity is to experience grace. From the Kegon Sutra, we hear, "The Buddha, pure and like space, without shape or form pervades all."[10] The Jewish Kaballah teaches, "Be aware that God fashioned everything and is within everything. There is nothing else."[11] Jesus said, "I am the light that is over all things. I am all: From me all has come forth, and to me all has reached. Split a piece of wood; I am there. Lift up the stone, and you will find me there."[12] Taoists say, "The great Tao flows everywhere." And in a dazzling metaphor, Hildegard of Bingen says, "All living creatures are, so to speak, sparks from the radiation of God's brilliance, and these sparks emerge from God like the rays of the sun."[13]

The ethic that derives from understanding the universality of our own divine natures is called Love. Compassion, in all the world's spiritual traditions, describes this unity: a felt relationship, with all others, but especially with those who may need our help. It is passionate and caring, and much more about responding to a sense of oneness with the rest of humanity than about meeting the demands of a particular religious commandment. When compassion is not obstructed by narcissism, materialism, and dualistic thinking, it naturally flows from a deep well of human and divine energies. Look for the common threads of humanity, compassion, and spirituality. As you become more and more mindful of our elemental unity, you will be opening yourself to the experience of ordinary grace.

7. Understand and celebrate the differences between people. Focusing on the underlying essence of the great traditions should not mean erasing the differences between them, or creating a homogenized philosophy. There are meaningful differences between the great faiths of mankind about the precise nature of God, the relationship between man and God, the nature of the soul, and what happens to us after death. These differences in the doctrines, rituals, and histories give each tradition its own unique identity and are of great importance to believers in those faiths.

The Roman Catholic monk Bede Griffiths lived for thirty-five years in an ashram in India, where he studied with a small community of people who were of different faiths but were one in their desire to know the truth. He likened the world's great formal religions—Hinduism, Buddhism, Judaism, Islam, and Christianity—to fingers on a hand. If we look at the fingers themselves, we see only that they are very separate. But if we follow them down to their roots, we can understand that they all come from the same hand.[14] "The function of comparative religion," he wrote, "is to discern this essential Truth, this divine Mystery beyond speech and thought, in the language-forms of each religious tradition, from the most primitive tribal traditions to the most advanced world religions. In each tradition the one divine Reality, the one eternal Truth is present, but it is hidden under symbols, symbols of word and gesture, of ritual and dance and song, of poetry and music, art and architecture, of custom and convention, of law and morality, of philosophy and theology."[15]

In the same way, the beauty of ordinary grace is that it revels in and praises all of creation. In order to truly help others, one must not only tolerate but also embrace the individuality of others. One must emphasize the underlying unity of all of life while at the same time celebrating our differences. The thirteenth-century monk Thomas Aquinas reminded us that "diversity is the perfection of the universe."

8. *Put belief into action.* Some people derive their faith in humanity from a belief in God. Others eschew religion and instead set their compasses by a strong sense of social justice. Whatever the source of one's beliefs, endless reflecting on one's convictions pales in importance compared to acting on them. Those who express grace seem to make an effortless transition from belief into action. Helping others seems natural to them—like breathing.

Psychiatrist and prolific writer Robert Coles has researched the moral development of children and believes that in order to help children develop morally, it is critical to transform nouns into verbs. The idea that virtue is a function not just of goodness but of habit is one that was endorsed by Plato, Aristotle,

Aquinas, Augustine, Bacon, Hegel, and James, among others. Generosity, kindness, thoughtfulness, sensitivity, and compassion are not intended to be exalted ideas, but rather modes of behavior. "Character," to Coles, is nothing more than the sum of our imagined plans turned into action. "Take those nouns that denote good moral traits, and with the help of your sons and daughters try to convert them into verbs: tasks to accomplish, plans for action, to be followed by the actual work of doing," he writes.[16]

9. *Find grace in small things.* For many of us, the hardest thing about finding our way to grace is that it seems so daunting. But as we've seen, it's possible to find generosity and compassion in even the smallest gestures. I remember a story about Karl Menninger, the psychiatrist and writer who established the Menninger Foundation in Topeka, Kansas. Dr. Menninger was asked to visit a widow who had been depressed for several years. When he went to her home, he found her sitting slumped in a chair, and she admitted that she had been depressed since her husband's death many years before. Her house was dark and quiet. But Menninger observed that she grew beautiful African violets. He wrote an unusual prescription: it instructed her to read her local newspaper every day and send one of her violets to someone in her community who had experienced a significant event: the birth of a baby, a marriage, a graduation, or a death in the family. Within a month, this woman called and told him that her life had changed dramatically. She had become excited about life.

She said that every time she sent a violet, people responded to her. They appreciated her kindness and reciprocated by sending cookies or a thank-you note, or by paying a visit to let her know she was appreciated. She soon became known as "the violet lady," and lived the rest of her life surrounded by new friends.

Like the leaves of the tamarind tree, all of these little acts contribute to a canopy that protects everyone. The writer Alice Walker emphasizes the point: "We should not be discouraged when our acts are small, when our acts are not grand, heroic things. We have to regain our belief in the power of what is small."[17]

10. *Build on your immediate, personal connections to others.* The expression of ordinary grace starts most naturally with people one is connected to: our families, our friends, our co-workers, our neighbors. Look at these important relationships. What do they mean to you? Can they be built into something stronger, more solid, deeper? By bringing grace into our relationships with those closest to us, we can learn to expand our circle of love into an ever-widening sphere and can begin to welcome the stranger in.

All of the people I interviewed described an abiding sense of unity with all others, of a love that the Greeks called *agape* and defined as "selfless," the love that Christians hold to be the most important teaching of Jesus. These people express what Buddhists refer to as *bodhichitta*, an awakened, softened heart, and a spontaneous feeling of compassion, of "suffering with" another without thinking about it. This is what Schopenhauer called the "breakthrough of the metaphysical realization," the understanding that separation from the rest of life is just an illusion. Mythologist Joseph Campbell described the way that compassion arises from such feelings of connection: "It is an immediate participation in the suffering of another to such a degree that you forget yourself and your own safety and spontaneously do what is necessary."[18]

11. Model good behavior. Reinforcing moral ideas is a good way of encouraging children to become virtuous adults. But children learn mostly by what they see and hear, which is why parents and other adults teach children the most valuable lessons by modeling good behavior. Not a single person I interviewed said that their parents taught morality in a formal way. As children, these people simply watched their parents living their values, and in so doing, they learned the difference between right and wrong and the importance of caring for other people.

Although there will always be differences of opinion among thoughtful people about which values should be taught and how they are to be expressed, there's little doubt that teaching moral values in school is an effective way to help a child develop into a healthy, virtuous adult. Schools can easily refrain from focusing on controversial moral issues like prayer in public schools, abortion, and the death penalty, and concentrate instead on universally accepted values such as honesty, compassion, generosity, courage, loyalty, perseverance, respect for others, and the importance of contributing to the community.[19] Recent research in 176 public schools that included a values curriculum demonstrated a 77 percent decline in behavior problems, a 68 percent increase in attendance, and a 64 percent decrease in vandalism. In other schools that included such teaching, teenage pregnancy went down, disciplinary actions were reduced, and academic test scores went up.[20]

Nevertheless, the old adage "Do as I say, not as I do," is a clear warning about what doesn't work. Parents and teachers may carry on and on about the great spiritual traditions and the classic philosophical arguments on morality, but children will emulate what they *observe.* You can read to your child about George Washington and his honesty when he told his father that he'd cut down the cherry tree. If your child observes you lying to someone, the story will soon be forgotten, and your lie will be remembered forever. The sixteenth-century Swiss alchemist Paracelsus reminded us to "believe in the works, not the words; words are an empty shell, but the works show you the master."[21]

In the book *The Moral Intelligence of Children,* Robert Coles makes a case for setting an example for children through our own actions: "We grow morally as a consequence of learning how to be with others, how to behave in this world, a learning prompted by taking to heart what we have seen and heard. The child is a witness; the child is an ever-attentive witness of grown-up morality—or lack thereof; the child looks and looks for clues as to how one ought to behave, and finds them galore as we parents and teachers go about our lives, making choices, addressing people, showing in action our rock-bottom assumptions, desires, and values, and thereby telling these young observers much more than we may realize."[22]

12. *Begin now.* Goethe wrote: "Whatever you can do or dream, you can begin it. Boldness has genius, power, and magic in it. Begin it now." Don't wait until you are very old and changes become more difficult to make in your life. Don't be on your deathbed wishing that you had lived differently. Elisabeth Kübler-Ross has spent her lifetime studying death, dying, and the transpersonal; she offers this same advice. She says, "There is within each of us a potential for goodness beyond our imagining; for giving which seeks no reward; for listening without judgment; for loving unconditionally. . . . Everything is bearable when there is love. My wish is that you try to give more people more love."[23] Make a decision today to enter into the stream of grace that flows all around you.

If you've decided that you would like to demonstrate your compassion, but you don't think you have the time or even enough information about how to go about it, think again. Every local newspaper offers many opportunities to give a great deal of time, or just a little, to others. Local United Way organizations can suggest many ways of serving your community.[24] The Points of Light Foundation, founded in 1990, is a non-profit, nonpartisan organization devoted to matching people with volunteer opportunities that fit their lives and their schedules.[25] Even in the smallest moments of every day we are met with chances to demonstrate our compassion and kindness. At this moment you have almost finished reading this book. What will you do when you're done and have put it back on the shelf? Is there something that you could do right now, this very moment, to make the world a better place? "Begin it now," Goethe advised.

13. Understand that you are not alone. In the spring of 1996, John Wilson, the publisher of the remarkably popular though somewhat esoteric magazine *WoodenBoat*, started another magazine, one he felt dealt with "a more important idea." *Hope* was born out of the realization that many people are searching for "good news" and could benefit from stories that remind them that compassion and empathy are alive and well in the world.[26]

Like *Hope* magazine, many mainstream publications, books on the best-seller list, Hollywood films, and modern music are increasingly emphasizing spirituality, generosity, and goodness. Just like you, millions of people are searching for a new metaphor, a new way of looking at their lives, and a new cosmology that speaks to the heart as well as the mind. As we cross over into a new millennium, we find ourselves in the midst of a paradigm shift, a change of heart—a metanoia—and the evidence for it is all around. More and more people are experiencing a call to awaken, to bring spirit into their lives, to feel the presence of the divine. The great works of philosophers, the oral traditions and myths of indigenous cultures, and the sacred texts of the world's religions have described an unambiguous path toward meaning, passion, and the radiant experience of the spirit. Each moment is ripe with the opportunity to reach out with love to others and to extend our compassion to all sentient beings and to the earth herself. Lakota Sioux shaman Black Elk makes clear the path to grace when he says, "Like the grasses showing tender faces to each other, thus should we do, for this was the wish of the Grandfathers of the World."

Postscript

The day will come when, after harnessing the winds, the tides,

and gravitation, we shall harness for God the energies

of love. And on that day, for the second time in the

history of the world, man will have discovered fire.[1]

—Pierre Teilhard de Chardin, *The Evolution of Chastity*

I t's an early February morning, before seven o'clock, and I'm driving up the Garden State Parkway, in New Jersey, to Clark, where I'll have a chance to meet with the volunteers of the Yes, We Care mobile soup kitchen. It's well below freezing—the radio has reported nine degrees, but the wind chill makes it feel even colder. I'm wondering what I've gotten myself into by choosing to write about ordinary grace, but my aunt Mary Gallagher knows these people—she was involved in the creation of the group, and an active participant until she moved out of the area. She's assured me that my time will be well spent.

I find the Lutheran church where the group convenes, makes

the soup, and packs the truck. I enter through a back door that leads directly to the kitchen. Inside there are massive pots of chicken noodle soup simmering on the stove. It smells delicious, and just the sight of the steam rising from the soup feels warm and inviting. I meet Cathy Friedman—all her friends call her Ziggy, a holdover from her maiden name, Zigglehoffer—who is a nurse on the eleven-to-seven shift and has come here straight from work. She's a New Jersey transplant, she says, originally from a big Ohio family with six older brothers.

I want to know what motivates her to leave directly from a long night's work and come to make soup for people she doesn't even know. She attends this Lutheran church but doesn't consider herself particularly religious. Nevertheless, she has a strong belief that all people should do something for their community. "There's a lot of things that churches teach that I just don't think are right. People get too hung up on the differences between them. I mean, who cares whether someone is black or white, gay or straight, working or homeless? Those things just don't make any difference. We're all the same and we've all been taught the Golden Rule. I'm a very lucky person, I have a lot to be thankful for, and I should give something back."

She tells me about the group of people who, inspired by Dr. Sanford "Sonny" Fineman, a neurosurgeon at Union Hospital, got together in December 1992. Ziggy describes Sonny as "an amazing person," someone who goes right from the operating room to the soup kitchen. Back in 1992, he was looking for a way to give something to the community, and he came up with a plan. He bought a 1977 Lance Bread truck, added a few industrial metal tables in the back, and loaded it with food. On a Monday night, Sonny, Ziggy, my aunt Mary, and other volunteers began to make sandwiches, pack up fruit and bread, and gather coats, gloves, scarves, and other things that people living in poverty need but don't have.

I'm riding in the back of the same rumbling truck, which is now filled with hundreds of bags that have been packed with sandwiches and fruit. There's a pile of coats and jackets that I'm using for a seat. "The passenger door has a tendency to fly open," Sonny tells me, so I'm quite happy sitting in the back.

Hoping not to seem too forward, I mention delicately that it would be quite easy for a man in his position to make a generous donation to a community service organization. "No, that doesn't cut it," he says. "This is just a small way of giving back. That's not a cliché but a reality statement. I grew up in Philadelphia. We lived in Center City and when we went out to dinner we had to go past lots of flophouses. Homelessness was apparent even then. My mom used to give coats out, and always told my father to give someone a couple of bucks when they were asking for money. I remember thinking, even as a little kid, how can it be that people don't have a place to live, not even one room? I saw people sleeping on steam grates to keep warm."

Later, while working as a resident at Jefferson Hospital in Philadelphia, he tended to an older man in the emergency room. "I talked with him and he was well-spoken and very knowledgeable. It broke down any stereotypes or misconceptions I might have ever held about homeless people. There but for the grace of God goes any one of us. There are so many problems—addictions to drugs and alcohol, lots of mental illness—but underneath it all we are human beings and we are connected."

Sonny is very proud of the fact that the Yes, We Care mobile soup kitchen is fully staffed by volunteers. He pays for the insurance, gas, and repairs to the truck, and all the money raised through donations goes to buy food. On Monday nights, the kitchen is filled with people—teenagers, doctors, nurses, schoolteachers—who make sandwiches and pack the truck. "We start about seven and make hundreds of sandwiches, and are still finished by eight. It doesn't take that much time to be involved. Once people see how easy it is they want to come back for more."

We've left Clark, and drive into a section of Elizabeth that has been decaying for years. Graffiti is painted over almost every building, storefronts are boarded up, and everything looks very old and tired. It is the kind of inner-city neighborhood that feels dangerous and unfamiliar. Sonny looks around and says, "For some people here, this will be their only meal of the day. How can that be in a country as rich as ours? Did you know that thirty-seven million dollars were spent on inauguration events in Washington? How many people would that feed, do you think?"

"There is a universality in everyone. In Judaism there is a concept of *tsedaka*—a giving of oneself. I'm a big believer in that. There are things that we can do to praise God, and one of them is helping our fellow man. As a doctor, I can tell you that poverty and sickness transcend all racial or religious bounds. I want my children to understand how important it is to reach out. They come and work on the truck during the summer and other vacations from school. They're learning from what they see. They learn about being thankful for all the blessings in their lives, and the importance of reaching out with compassion. They turned down a chance to go scuba-diving last summer in order to do community service in a Third World country. My wife, Arlene, and I are so proud of them and the choice that they made."

We pull to a stop on an empty street. Ziggy and another volunteer named Jimmy pull up—they've come in Ziggy's car, which is loaded with clothes to be distributed. Within minutes, the street becomes alive with people emerging from behind buildings and out of alleys. Sonny opens the back door of the truck and greets two men, regulars who help with the distribution of the food and keep order in the crowd when necessary. Jimmy is handing out the bags of sandwiches. Sonny is looking at a bruise on a man's arm—giving curbside medical advice and fixing minor problems is just part of his work here. Ziggy is lining up styrofoam cups and plastic spoons. I'm part of the ladle crew, and begin to hand out cups of the hot soup, still steaming in the nine-degree air. There is quite a bit of jostling, people nudging their way to the front of the line. It's the end of the month, so even those who receive a small amount of money from social services have spent it. It's a big crowd today, Ziggy tells me. There must be almost two hundred people surrounding the truck.

Most of the people close in are men, most are black, and all of them have shaking hands and bloodshot eyes, evidence of their addictions. "We don't judge anybody," Sonny had told me on the ride over. "Some people told us that we were being used for free food by people who had money to buy some. But we don't care. Anyone who comes up for a cup of soup or a sandwich has some reason to be there."

I'm serving the soup as fast as I can. Weathered hands are reaching out, some in filthy woolen gloves full of holes and tears. And then suddenly the crowd backs away slightly from the truck. It's an almost imperceptible movement, but I watch as an old white woman is revealed standing at the rear of the crowd. She looks to be around ninety, though I know living in this kind of poverty shows itself and it's possible that she is seventy, maybe even sixty. She has a half-there look that I've seen in severely psychotic patients in mental hospitals. Her mouth is caved in—she has no teeth—and she's making little kissing sounds and talking out loud to no one in particular. She's wearing a coat many sizes too large and her hands are lost in the sleeves, which makes her arms appear disproportionately long, like a monkey's. A black wool hat is hanging part on, part off her head, and her gray hair looks electric as it sticks out in all directions. If she weren't so sad-looking, her appearance would almost be comical: another crazy Carol Burnett or Lily Tomlin character.

As the crowd clears a path for her, I watch as the shaking hands that had been grabbing up the soup containers a minute earlier begin to point toward her. I see the faces of these people and their message is clear. They are telling me to make sure that she gets some soup first, before it's gone. I am overwhelmed by this simple kindness. The woman makes her way over to me, through the parted crowd, and I ladle some of the hot soup into a cup for her. She takes it with both hands, saying nothing. She turns and the crowd folds back in around her.

We came here to give something but left, instead, with a most remarkable gift. Here, even in the most desperate and despairing of circumstances, grace was present, and it flowed over all of us.

Notes

Introduction

1. Information on Thomas Cannon is from Philip Smith, "Retired Mailman with Heart of Gold Hands Out $81,000 of His Own Money," *National Enquirer*, May 9, 1995.

2. Information on Eunice Lewis is from Vicki Lewis, "Thumbs Up!" in "The Compass," *Virginian-Pilot*, July 20, 1995.

3. Information on Trenkle and Sill is from Mara Stanley, "A Pair of Unlikely Friends," *Virginian-Pilot*, June 12, 1995.

4. Hannah Arendt, *Eichmann in Jerusalem: A Report on the Banality of Evil*. New York: Penguin, 1994 (originally published New York: Viking, 1963), p. 276.

5. Ralph Waldo Emerson, in *Emerson in His Journals*, ed. Joel Porte. Cambridge, MA: Harvard University Press, 1984.

Chapter 1

1. The Retired and Senior Volunteer Program is one of three programs of the National Senior Service Corps operating under the Corporation for National Service (CNS), which was chartered by Congress in 1993 to provide a broad range of opportunities for community service to all people. In addition to RSVP, the National Senior Service Corps oversees the Foster Grandparent Program and Senior Companions, which assists elderly people to live independently. For more information about the National Senior Service Corps, call 1-800-424-8867; or visit the website: http://www.cns.gov/senior.html.

2. For information about becoming a participant in the National Marrow Donor Program, call your local chapter of the American Red Cross or 1-800-MARROW-7. The initial procedure is nothing more than a simple blood test. Most people will never be called on to donate bone marrow.

3. William Blake, "The Marriage of Heaven and Hell" and "A Memorable Fancy" (pl. 14), in *The Portable Blake*, ed. Alfred Kazin. New York: Penguin, 1946, p. 258.

4. Huston Smith, *The Religions of Man.* New York: HarperCollins, 1986, p. 156.

5. Cited in Ronald S. Miller et al., *As Above So Below.* New York: Jeremy P. Tarcher, p. 109.

Chapter 2

1. The words "original sin" do not appear anywhere in the Bible, although theologians who accept the doctrine argue that it is strongly

implied by Paul and John. Augustine in the fourth century was the first to define the construct of original sin as being passed from generation to generation by the act of procreation (the term "original sin" was coined by Tertullian, a second-century theologian). The idea that we are born with sin was reasserted in a clearly Augustinian form by Martin Luther and John Calvin in the sixteenth century. Jewish tradition does not recognize the concept, despite the Jewish people's familiarity with the story of Genesis a thousand years before Christianity.

2. *Confession of Faith,* Presbyterian Church of Scotland, August 1, 1560.

3. Elaine Pagels, *Adam, Eve, and the Serpent.* New York: Vintage, 1988, p. xxvi. See also Bill Moyers, *Genesis: A Living Conversation.* New York: Doubleday, 1996; this book is a companion to the public television series of the same name.

4. Sigmund Freud, *Civilization and Its Discontents.* New York: W.W. Norton, 1961 (originally published 1930).

5. William J. Bennett, *The Book of Virtues.* New York: Simon & Schuster, 1993, p. 12.

6. Hildegard of Bingen, *Illuminations,* comm. Matthew Fox. Santa Fe, NM: Bear & Company, 1985.

7. Charles Hirshberg, "Primal Compassion," photographs by Robert Allison, *Life,* November 1996, pp. 78–82.

8. Human beings share 98.4 percent of their DNA sequences with chimpanzees and more than 92 percent with old world monkeys (see R. J. Britten, "Rates of DNA Sequence Evolution Differ Between Taxonomic Groups," *Science,* 1986, 23:1393–98). The idea that man was descended from the "apes" caused quite a controversy, which continues to this day among those who believe in creationism, that is, a literal interpretation of biblical passages. In June 1860, the wife of the bishop of Worcester responded to the idea that humans and apes had some common ancestor by exclaiming, "My dear, descended from the apes! Let us hope it is not true, but if it is,

let us pray that it will not become generally known!" (Richard E. Leakey and Roger Lewin, *Origins.* New York: E. P. Dutton, 1977, p. 21).

9. Shoji Itakura, "Differentiated Responses to Different Human Conditions by Chimpanzees," *Perceptual and Motor Skills,* vol. 79, no. 3, pt. 1 (Dec. 1994), pp. 1288–90.

10. R. M. Yerkes and A. W. Yerkes, *The Great Apes: A Study of Anthropoid Life.* New Haven, CT: Yale University Press, 1929, p. 297.

11. Frans de Waal, *Good-Natured: The Origins of Right and Wrong in Humans and Other Animals.* Cambridge, MA: Harvard University Press, 1996, p. 58.

12. Ibid., p. 19. See also Frans de Waal, *Peacemaking Among Primates.* Cambridge, MA: Harvard University Press, 1989.

13. Martin L. Hoffman, "Developmental Synthesis of Affect and Cognition and Its Interplay for Altruistic Motivation," *Developmental Psychology,* vol. 11 (1975), pp. 607–22.

14. Leslie Brothers, "A Biological Perspective on Empathy," *American Journal of Psychiatry,* vol. 146 (1989), p. 16.

15. Carolyn Zahn-Waxler, Marian Radke-Yarrow, Elizabeth Wagner, and Michael Chapman, "Development of Concern for Others," *Developmental Psychology,* vol. 28 (1992), pp. 126–36.

16. J. Madeleine Nash, "Fertile Minds," *Time,* February 3, 1997, pp. 48–56.

17. Jane Allyn Piliavin and Hong-Wen Charng, "Altruism: A Review of Recent Theory and Research," *Annual Review of Sociology,* vol. 16 (1990), pp. 27–65.

18. Stephen Foehr, "A Culture of Sharing," *New Age Journal,* Jan./Feb. 1997.

19. Desmond Morris, *The Human Animal.* New York: Crown, 1994, p. 88.

20. Matthew Fox, *Original Blessing.* Santa Fe, NM: Bear & Company, 1983.

21. The Dalai Lama, *Ethics for the Next Millennium.* New York: Riverhead, 1999.

22. Julian of Norwich, cited in Matthew Fox and Rupert Sheldrake, *Natural Grace.* New York: Doubleday, 1966, p. 55.

23. William Eckhardt, *Compassion: Toward a Science of Value.* Oakville, Ontario, 1973, pp. 4f. Cited in Fox, *Original Blessing,* p. 50.

24. G. K. Chesterton, "Defendant," in *The Collected Works of G. K. Chesterton,* Marlin, Swan, and Rabatin, eds. Fort Collins, CO: Ignatius Press, 1987.

Chapter 3

1. For more information contact:

   Flow from the Heart Foundation

   4025 East Chandler Boulevard, #70-A16

   Phoenix, AZ 85044

   1-602-759-1984; fax 1-602-759-3956

   Website: http://www.arastar.net/org/flow/

The website was set up and is maintained for the foundation through the generosity of Arastar World Products, an importing and Internet-marketing corporation.

2. John W. Allman, "Showing a Little Kindness," Pensacola *News Journal,* March 7, 1997.

3. Thomas Merton, *Run to the Mountain: The Journals of Thomas Merton,* vol. 1, 1939–1941. New York: HarperCollins, 1995, p. 304.

Chapter 4

1. Jelaluddin Rumi, "Bismillah," in *The Essential Rumi,* trans. Coleman Barks with John Moyne. New York: HarperCollins, 1995, p. 70.

2. Thich Nhat Hanh, *Living Buddha, Living Christ.* New York: Riverhead, 1995, p. 11.

3. *The Gospel of Thomas: The Hidden Sayings of Jesus,* trans. and comm. Marvin Meyer. New York: HarperCollins, 1992, p. 35. The Gospel of Thomas was discovered in 1945, part of the Coptic texts of the Nag Hammadhi library.

4. *The Essential Kabbalah: The Heart of Jewish Mysticism,* trans. and comm. Daniel C. Matt. San Francisco: HarperSanFrancisco, 1995, p. 26.

5. If you are interested in reading a wonderful book about the experiences of dying and coming back to life through organ transplantation, I urge you to read Frank Maier with Ginny Maier, *Sweet Reprieve.* New York: Crown, 1991.

6. About 30 percent of cadaver organ donations cross racial lines. Matching tissue types between people of different races is not rare, but cross-racial organ transplants from living donors is very uncommon. Recent research has shown that kidney transplants between living blood relatives are no more successful than those between living, unrelated donors. Both are more successful than when kidneys are transplanted from cadavers. Five years after kidney transplant, only 71 percent of cadaver transplants were still functioning, compared to 83 percent of those transplanted from living, related donors, and 86 percent of living, unrelated-donor transplants.

7. Claire Sylvia with William Novak, *A Change of Heart.* Boston: Little, Brown, 1997.

8. Amy Doggette, personal communication, July 7, 1997; R. G. Simmons, S. D. Klein, and R. L. Simmons, *The Gift of Life: The Social and Psychological Impact of Organ Transplantation.* New York: John Wiley & Sons, 1977.

9. Frederick Buechner, cited in Frederic and Mary Ann Brussat, *Spiritual*

Literacy: Reading the Sacred in Everyday Life. New York: Charles Scribner's Sons, 1996, p. 261.

For more information about obtaining an organ donor card or living kidney donation, contact:

UNOS (United Network for Organ Sharing)

1100 Boulders Parkway, Suite 500

Richmond, VA 23225

1-800-243-DONOR (243-6667)

Website: http://204.127.237.11:80/

Chapter 5

1. Jelaluddin Rumi, *Jewels of Remembrance: Rumi,* sel. and trans. Camille and Kabir Helminski. Putney, VT: Threshold Books, 1996, p. 9.

Chapter 6

1. Clarissa Pinkola Estés, *Women Who Run With the Wolves.* New York: Ballantine, 1992, p. 120.

2. See "Black Youth Volunteering More Than Other Citizens," *Jet,* vol. 83, no. 10 (Dec. 28, 1992, and Jan. 4, 1993), p. 28.

3. Information on Melvin Elliott is from Nancy Lewis, "Youth Spends Summer Helping the Elderly," *Virginian-Pilot,* Aug. 24, 1996, p. B3.

4. Information on Pizza-Ria! is from Larry W. Brown, "Teens Deliver on Promise of Pizza to Public Housing," *Virginian-Pilot,* Sept. 20, 1996, p. B1.

Chapter 7

1. For information contact:

   Physicians for Peace

   229 West Bute Street, Suite 820

   Norfolk, VA USA 23510

   1-757-625-7569; fax 1-757-625-7680

2. Richard Andrews did not win the election, but he conducted a fair race that brought many issues into public discussion—his original and primary objective.

3. The First Team website address is: http://wpmcl.wpafb.af.mil/hideout/home.htm.

Chapter 8

1. Judy Quinn, "Hotly Contested . . . by One: Dutton Drops $500K Offer for Thriller After Misrepresented Auction," *Publishers Weekly*, June 2, 1997, p. 25.

2. Carl Jung, "The Persona as a Segment of the Collective Psyche," in *Collected Works*, vol. 7. Princeton, NJ: Princeton University Press, 1953, par. 246. See also Robert Hopcke, *Persona*. Boston: Shambhala, 1995.

3. Marion Woodman, *Dreams: Language of the Soul* (audiotape). Boulder, CO: Sounds True Recordings, 1991.

4. See Connie Zweig and Jeremiah Abrams, eds., *Meeting the Shadow*. Los Angeles: Jeremy P. Tarcher, 1991.

5. For an excellent discussion of this, see Anne A. Simpkinson, "Soul Betrayal," *Common Boundary*, Nov./Dec. 1996, pp. 24–37.

6. Anthony Stevens, *On Jung*. London: Penguin, 1991, p. 43.

7. Jelaluddin Rumi, *The Essential Rumi*, trans. Coleman Barks with John Moyne. San Francisco: HarperSanFrancisco, 1995.

8. Kahlil Gibran, *The Prophet.* New York: Alfred A. Knopf, 1969, p. 326.

9. For information, write to or call:

Jonathan's Dream c/o GHJCC

335 West Bloomfield Avenue

West Hartford, CT 06117

1-860-654-5700

10. Rainer Maria Rilke, *Duino Elegies,* trans. C. F. MacIntyre. Berkeley: University of California Press, 1940; repr. 1989, no. 8, li. 75.

Chapter 9

1. Eknath Easwaran, *Your Life Is Your Message.* New York: Hyperion, 1992, p. 12.

2. Pierre Teilhard de Chardin, *The Divine Milieu.* New York: Harper & Row, 1960, p. 15.

3. Cited in Marion Woodman and Elinor Dickson, *Dancing in the Flames.* Boston: Shambhala, 1996, p. 201.

4. James P. Brehony, "If You Listen" (unpublished poem), 1997.

5. Cited in Robert Coles, *The Call of Service.* New York: Houghton Mifflin, 1993, p. 39.

6. Wayne Muller, *How Then Shall We Live?* New York: Bantam, 1996, p. 25.

7. Cited in Caryle Hirshberg and Marc Ian Barasch, *Remarkable Recovery.* New York: Riverhead, 1995, p. 209.

8. Henry David Thoreau, *Walden.* Princeton, NJ: Princeton University Press, 1989.

9. Marion Woodman, "The Conscious Feminine," *Common Boundary,* vol. 7, no. 2 (March/April 1989). Reprinted in Marion Woodman, *Conscious Femininity.* Toronto: Inner City, 1993, pp. 88–89.

10. Cited in many sources, including Ram Dass and Mirabai Bush, *Compassion in Action.* New York: Bell Tower, 1992, p. 102.

11. Abraham Maslow, *Toward a Psychology of Being.* New York: Van Nostrand Reinhold, 1968, p. 209.

12. Information on Common Cents is from Colin Greer, "Make Pennies Count," *Parade,* Aug. 11, 1996, pp. 8–9.

13. The Keshia Thomas story is documented in *People,* July 8, 1996, p. 86.

14. Chögyam Trungpa, cited in Jack Kornfield, *A Path with Heart.* New York: Bantam, 1993, pp. 222–23.

Chapter 10

1. Jimmy Carter, *Living Faith.* New York: Times Books/Random House, 1996, p. 4.

2. Bernard Glassman and Rick Fields, *Instructions to the Cook.* New York: Bell Tower, 1996, p. 8.

3. The Dalai Lama, *World in Harmony.* Berkeley, CA: Parallax, 1992.

4. Kathleen A. Brehony, *Awakening at Midlife.* New York: Riverhead, 1996.

5. Carlos Castaneda, *The Teachings of Don Juan: A Yaqui Way of Knowledge.* Berkeley: University of California Press, 1968.

6. Pema Chödrön, *Start Where You Are.* Boston: Shambhala, 1994, p. 3.

7. Joe Dominguez and Vicki Robin, *Your Money or Your Life.* New York: Penguin, 1992.

8. Elaine St. James, *Living the Simple Life.* New York: Hyperion, 1996. See also Duane Elglin, *Voluntary Simplicity.* New York: William Morrow, 1993; and Sarah Ban Breathnach, *Simple Abundance.* New York: Warner Books, 1995.

9. Huston Smith, *The Religions of Man.* New York: HarperCollins, 1986, p. 5.

10. *A First Zen Reader*, comp. and trans. Trevor Leggett. Tokyo: Charles E. Tuttle, 1960, p. 46.

11. *The Essential Kaballah: The Heart of Jewish Mysticism*, trans. and comm. Daniel C. Matt. San Francisco: HarperSanFrancisco, 1995, p. 25.

12. *The Gospel of Thomas: The Hidden Sayings of Jesus*, trans. and comm. Marvin Meyer. New York: HarperCollins, 1992, p. 55.

13. Hildegard of Bingen, *Illuminations*, comm. Matthew Fox. Santa Fe, NM: Bear & Company, 1985, p. 47.

14. Cited in Matthew Fox and Rupert Sheldrake, *Natural Grace*. New York: Doubleday, 1996, p. 113.

15. Bede Griffiths, *Return to the Center*. Springfield, IL: Templegate, 1976, p. 71.

16. Robert Coles, *The Moral Intelligence of Children*. New York: Random House, 1997, p. 16.

17. Anne A. Simpkinson, "Freeing the Seed," *Common Boundary*, vol. 15, no. 2 (March/April 1997), pp. 20–25. See also Alice Walker, *Anything We Love Can Be Saved*. New York: Random House, 1997.

18. Cited in Frederic and Mary Ann Brussat, *Spiritual Literacy: Reading the Sacred in Everyday Life*. New York: Charles Scribner's Sons, 1996, p. 91.

19. The Virtues Project, initiated in 1991 to empower individuals, families, and schools, has identified fifty-two virtues that are consistent with our country's moral ideals:

Assertiveness	Courage	Excellence	Gentleness
Caring	Courtesy	Faithfulness	Helpfulness
Cleanliness	Creativity	Flexibility	Honesty
Compassion	Detachment	Forgiveness	Honor
Confidence	Determination	Friendliness	Humility
Consideration	Enthusiasm	Generosity	Idealism

Joyfulness	Modesty	Reliability	Tact
Justice	Obedience	Respect	Thankfulness
Kindness	Orderliness	Responsibility	Tolerance
Love	Patience	Reverence	Trust
Loyalty	Peacefulness	Self-discipline	Trustworthiness
Mercy	Prayerfulness	Service	Truthfulness
Moderation	Purposefulness	Steadfastness	Unity

The Virtues Project has published *The Virtues Guide,* and offers other material on teaching virtues. For more information or to order material, contact:

Virtues Communications

PO Box 18078

Fountain Hills, AZ 85269

1-800-850-0714; fax 1-602-816-0716

E-mail: VirtuesCom@aol.com

Website: http://www.virtuesproject.com/

20. Kathleen Kennedy Townsend, "Why Johnny Can't Tell Right from Wrong: The Most Important Lesson Our Schools Don't Teach (Values)," *Washington Monthly,* vol. 24, no. 12 (Dec. 1992), pp. 29–33.

21. *Paracelsus: Selected Writings,* ed. Jolande Jacobi. Princeton, NJ: Princeton University Press, 1951, p. 101.

22. Coles, *Moral Intelligence,* p. 5.

23. Elisabeth Kübler-Ross, *The Wheel of Life: A Memoir of Living and Dying.* New York: Charles Scribner's Sons, 1997, p. 286.

24. For information, call your local United Way or the national number: 1-800-411-UWAY (411-8929).

25. The Points of Light Foundation can be reached by phone at 1-202-223-9186. The website address is: http://www.americaspromise.org.

26. For subscription information, contact:

Hope Magazine

PO Box 52241

Boulder, CO 80322-2241

1-800-273-7447

E-mail: subscribe@hopemag.com

Website: http://www.hopemag.com

Postscript

1. Pierre Teilhard de Chardin, *The Evolution of Chastity*, trans. René Hague. London: William Collins, 1972; reprinted in *On Love and Happiness.* San Francisco: Harper, 1984, p. 16.

Acknowledgments

In the philosophies of some Native American cultures, the deeply felt connections among members of a tribe are thought to be like pure strands of pulsating energy that create a shimmering web of relationships. Legend says that these bonds, these "strings of light," are so clear, so palpable, that some shamans can even see and touch them. Unlike these wise sorcerers, I cannot perceive these connections through my senses, but nonetheless I feel them in every moment through my heart. My life is profoundly graced by the love of my family and my family of friends. Surrounded by this powerful force, I take every step secure in the knowledge that I am, and always will be, a part of our tribe. I thank each and every one of you for your support and especially for the light and the love that you always bring into my life. You are my greatest blessings.

Acknowledgments

To my partners Sally Baker, Jan Hembree, and Caren Cross: Thank you not only for the extra coverage that gave me the opportunity to complete this book but also for your love. To my clients: My appreciation for your patience and heartfelt support.

To my literary agent, Lisa Ross: My deepest gratitude for your wise counsel, your good-natured enthusiasm, your confidence in me as a writer, and most important, your abiding friendship.

To Chris Knutsen and Cindy Spiegel, my editors at Riverhead Books: I extend my thanks for your unfailing support of this project. Your intelligence, skills, and commitment to this book are evident on every page.

My deepest appreciation to the remarkable people whose stories inform this book and to the millions of others like them around the globe, who bring grace, compassion, and love into the world. As Margaret Mead said, "Don't believe that even a small group of committed people cannot change the world. It's the only thing that ever has." Thank you.

Permissions

The author gratefully acknowledges permission to reprint the following:

Introduction: Thomas Cannon source material reprinted courtesy *National Enquirer.*

Chapters 1, 6: Source material from *Virginian-Pilot.* Reprinted with permission from *Virginian-Pilot,* Landmark Communications, Norfolk, Virginia.

Chapter 2: Hodi source material. Reprinted with permission of Stephen Foehr.

Chapter 3: Kathy Simmons source material. Reprinted with permission of Pensacola *News Journal,* Pensacola, Florida.

Chapter 4: Rumi, "You are so weak . . ." Translation © Coleman Barks. Reprinted with permission.

Permissions

Chapter 5: Rumi, "The most secure place . . ." Translation by Camille and Kabir Helminski. Reprinted with permission. Originally published in *Jewels of Remembrance* by Threshold Books, 139 Main Street, Brattleboro, Vermont 05301.

Chapter 8: "Hotly Contested . . . by One" source material. Reprinted with permission of *Publishers Weekly.*

Chapter 9: J. P. Brehony, "If You Listen." Unpublished poem © J. P. Brehony. Reprinted with permission.

"Make Pennies Count" source material. Reprinted with permission of Colin Greer. Reprinted with permission from *Parade,* copyright © 1996.

About the Author

Kathleen Brehony holds a Ph.D. in clinical psychology. She has been in private practice for fourteen years, specializing in periods of transitional development, including midlife and death and dying. Dr. Brehony is the author of *Awakening at Midlife: A Guide to Reviving Your Spirit, Re-creating Your Life, and Returning to Your Truest Self.* She divides her time between Virginia and Los Angeles.